THE SAVVY SUPERINTENDENT

LEADING INSTRUCTION TO THE TOP OF THE CLASS

Linda K. Wagner

Edited by Bert S. Friedman

Published in partnership with the
American Association of School Administrators

ROWMAN & LITTLEFIELD EDUCATION
A division of
ROWMAN & LITTLEFIELD PUBLISHERS, INC
Lanham • New York • Toronto • Plymouth, UK

Published in partnership with the American Association of
School Administrators

Published by Rowman & Littlefield Education
A division of Rowman & Littlefield Publishers, Inc.
A wholly owned subsidiary of
The Rowman & Littlefield Publishing Group, Inc.
4501 Forbes Boulevard, Suite 200, Lanham, Maryland 20706
http://www.rowmaneducation.com

Estover Road, Plymouth PL6 7PY, United Kingdom

British Library Cataloguing in Publication Information Available

Library of Congress Cataloging-in-Publication Data
Wagner, Linda K., 1965–
  The savvy superintendent : leading instruction to the top of the class /
Linda K. Wagner.
      p. cm.
  "Published in cooperation with the American Association of School
Administrators."
  Includes bibliographical references.
  ISBN 978-1-60709-720-4 (cloth : alk. paper) — ISBN 978-1-60709-721-1
(pbk. : alk. paper) — ISBN 978-1-60709-722-8 (electronic)
  1. School superintendents—United States. 2. School districts—United
States—Management. 3. Educational leadership—United States. I. American
Association of School Administrators. II. Title.
  LB2831.72.W34 2010
  371.2'011—dc22
                                                    2009053394

⊚ ™ The paper used in this publication meets the minimum requirements of
American National Standard for Information Sciences—Permanence of Paper
for Printed Library Materials, ANSI/NISO Z39.48-1992.

Printed in the United States of America

*This book is dedicated to
the many school superintendents
who strive to create bright futures
for students through education.*

They make a difference.

CONTENTS

ACKNOWLEDGMENTS

Special thanks to Bert Friedman on the completion of this manuscript. His writing and editorial abilities, and his command of the English language, made it possible for this book to appear before you in print. I am grateful for his encouragement, perseverance, and dedication.

INTRODUCTION

This is a guide for educational leaders who wish to create instructional leadership that results in effective schools. In this book, readers will learn the results of a study of the advice, stories, and experiences of top school superintendents from across the nation. Though their districts include rural, urban, and suburban environs and range in size from the very large to very small, each shares a commonality: a singular focus on creating student-focused school systems designed for educational success.

This book begins with foundational information about the structures required for success and moves into less obvious but no less important topics related to politics, assessment, and equity—issues critical to a superintendent's ability to positively impact instruction. Throughout the text are "Discussion Scenarios"—topics and questions to ponder or discuss with others.

A distinguished group of over fifty practicing and retired school and county superintendents was interviewed for this book. Consultants and county office administrators, who have all worked in the field of education, were interviewed as well.

The American Association of School Administrators (AASA) worked cooperatively with the author to arrange interviews with

AASA National Superintendents of the Year and finalists for this award from across the United States. Brief biographical sketches of the many contributors to this work can be found at the end of the book.

DEFINING INSTRUCTIONAL LEADERSHIP

Instructional leadership enabling improved student achievement requires intentional thought and action. It begins with a school or district leader who exhibits the characteristics necessary to build trust and capacity throughout the organization.

To be an "instructional leader," one must take intentional and deliberate steps to conceive a well-aligned vision of the goals to be achieved, and from this establish realistic, attainable, and measurable milestones of achievement.

Within this overarching structure, incremental, positive, and real improvements in the teaching and learning process can begin to take place. Gaps in student achievement can be filled in order to attain equity in the teaching and learning process. Instructional effectiveness is then measured via the study and review of student data, leading to re-teaching as needed.

State and federal legislation intended to increase accountability for student success has recently made it significantly more difficult to create systems capable of withstanding outside pressure while building upon the talents of educators to promote achievement from within.

The mandates of the No Child Left Behind Act, coupled with the upward trend of diagnoses leading to skyrocketing costs in specialized student services, cuts in funding, and myriad outside causatives can make school leaders question how to best shelter their staff and students from these pressures while concurrently encouraging a culture of continuous improvement. Building effective instructional leadership designed to improve student achievement is possible only when leaders have gained or deepened their understanding of successful and achievement-oriented instructional leadership.

ORGANIZATION OF THE BOOK

This book will take readers through the steps that lead to effective school change. From the important first steps of building capacity and trust and then following a well-managed and well-thought-out vision, instructional leaders will discover how to establish positive school cultures that promote successful teaching and learning.

Assessments of equity and academic success will serve as checkpoints for the school leader to examine his or her effectiveness. District leaders will learn what other practitioners are saying and doing relative to each step of the process and gain from the advice and experiences of others as a practical guide for their decision making.

STUDY PARTICIPANTS

John Aycock
Dr. Ralph Baker
Manny Barbara
Dr. Kent Bechler
John Beck
Richard Bray
Jim Brown
Noel Buehler
John Byerrum
Dr. Magdalena Carrillo-Mejia
Dr. Nancy Carroll
Dr. Joseph Condon
Susan Custer
Dr. Wendy Doty
Dr. Jody Dunlap
Henry Escobar
Dr. Dennis Fox
Robert Fraisse
Dr. Carmella Franco
Assemblywoman Dr. Jean Fuller

Roger Gallizzi
Tom Giampietro
Becci Gillespie
Dr. Gwen Gross
Dr. Jack Gyves
Dr. Mimi Hennessey
Robert Hodges
Terri Lancaster
Dr. Ronald Leon
Sandra Lyon
Dr. William J. Mathis
Dr. Sharon McGehee
Ned McNabb
Dr. Gary Mekeel
Dr. Henry Mothner, Ed.D.
Ken Noonan
Dr. Maria Ott
Sue Page
Dr. Krista D. Parent
Dr. James B. Phares

Dr. Juli Quinn

Dr. Sharon Robison

Dr. Darline Robles

Dr. Beverly Rohrer

Regina Rossall

Sherry Smith

Dr. Howard Sundberg

Dr. Louise Taylor

Sandra Thorstenson

Dr. Rene Townsend

Dr. David J. Verdugo

Dr. Jim Vidak

Dr. David Vierra

Renee Whitson

Dr. Marc Winger

Dr. Roberta Zapf

With Thanks To:

Steve Doyle

James B. Fernow

Bert S. Friedman

Lester Gerber

Linette Hodson

Bart Hoffman

Stephen Luhrs

Diane Parkins

Dr. Carol Roberts

Ross Swearingen

Joseph J. Wagner Jr.

Rebecca Wetzel

1

THE FIRST YEAR

This is not a job for the shy, the meek, or those who can't handle juggling. But when you look back, you can tell you made a difference. You effect so much change.

—Dr. Darline Robles

PREPARE YOUR PATHWAY TO THE SUPERINTENDENCY

There are as many varied journeys to the superintendency as there are superintendents. Some people prepare for the role with a great deal of planning, spending years lining up the "right" positions as they pursue their first superintendency. Others endure an arduous interview process, multiple panel interviews, dozens of reference checks, and visits to their current district from their prospective employer. And still others are thrust into a role for which they have not necessarily prepared, or even sought.

Some school districts contract with firms and outside consultants in a rigorous and well-thought-out search, and others might choose to undertake a superintendent search with very little notice. Surprisingly, some school boards might even decide to conduct no search at all. Imagine walking into a board meeting as assistant and leaving as superintendent. Individuals who are promoted in this way are likely to inherit a tumultuous situation, a difficult board, or both.

The large majority of superintendents find that their experience lies somewhere along the continuum. Most often, a person rises to the position of superintendent after someone notices their leadership skills and asks them to become a district leader.

Regardless of how or when the superintendent secures her first position or how much training and preparation she has had, "Nobody can be prepared to become superintendent," says Regina Rossall, a superintendent with over thirty years' experience in the field of education. "Superintendents take the job because they have the leadership skills to make a difference."

Being a superintendent involves visibility, accountability, conflict, and collaboration. To excel in the position involves both leading and following. A leader can make a significant difference for students, but he must do so while working within the constraints that come with boards composed of a small group of community members. A superintendent might feel that he can accomplish much, yet might instead find a laundry list of expectations and tasks waiting as soon as he accepts the position.

One reason it is impossible to fully prepare for the role of district leader is the differing requirements of the position; another is that the expectations of what it means to be a superintendent vary from district to district, and sometimes even from board member to board member.

The school board and the superintendent working together are referred to as the governance team. However, it is the board, and not the superintendent, who sets the direction for the district. A district leader's work is influenced and directed by matters ranging from the macroenvironmental impact of federal, state, and local politics to the microenvironmental effects of factors such as the demographics of a district, the preferences and requirements of each particular board, and even the passions and prejudices of each individual school board member.

The best preparation to be an effective instructional leader is simply to foster one's situational awareness: of the profession, the community, the district, and the board, and to develop a deep and abiding interest in, and understanding of, how best to meet the expectations of each.

One additional factor to consider is timing. Pace yourself. When I became a superintendent at the age of thirty-eight, my mentor kindly pointed out, "Becoming a superintendent at your age was your first mistake."

Balancing the business of the district with one's personal life is all a part of "the job." Get used to the reality of missed little league games and Girl Scout meetings, late dinners with your spouse, weekend phone calls, middle-of-the night emergencies, and public scrutiny. These, and the unanticipated and unexpected curveballs that life inevitably throws, are but a few examples of how being a superintendent can take its toll both personally and professionally.

Over time, a superintendent may learn to manage the stress and use it effectively, but more than one savvy longtime superintendent advised in interviews for this book that a late career move to the superintendency might be preferable. Many current and past leaders believe the superintendency should be the capstone of a long and successful career. "This job is a marathon, not a sprint," says Dr. Jack Gyves, a superintendent with twenty-five years of experience.

You should carefully consider how badly you want to endure the stress of the position before becoming a superintendent. Unless you are in the last ten years of your career, you should carefully consider the ramifications of ascending to the superintendency. Contemplating the feasibility and desirability of the job and the trade-offs you are willing and able to make after you have already accepted the position isn't fair to yourself, your family, or the district.

PLAN FOR GOOD BEGINNINGS

What might your first ninety days as a district leader look like?

During Franklin Delano Roosevelt's legendary "First 100 Days" from March 9 to June 16, 1933, fifteen legislative proposals were passed into law. Among other things, these provided for the creation

of the Federal Emergency Relief Administration, the Civilian Con-
servation Corps, the Reconstruction Finance Corporation, the Public
Works Administration, and the Tennessee Valley Authority.

In a short time, Congress gave the Federal Trade Commission
broad new regulatory powers and provided mortgage relief to mil-
lions of farmers and homeowners. Prohibition was repealed, and
the Agricultural Adjustment Act, the Economy Act, the Emergency
Banking Act, and Farm Credit Act were enacted.

You won't need to accomplish such far-reaching goals as a new
district leader; yet however you arrive in the district, whether hired
from the outside or promoted from within, a plan for the first ninety
days of your new administration is no less crucial. You might approach the board with a request to spend the first ninety days of
your superintendency gathering information. Goal-setting work can
be done thereafter.

Spend time talking with key employees, meeting with those in
the district with influence, opinions, and possibly also leadership or
power. Meet with city officials, parents, and parent groups, a variety
of employees, and the "movers and shakers" in town. Ask simple
questions:

1. What do you think is working in our district?
2. What do you think needs to be changed or adjusted?
3. What events, stories, programs, or protocols are held dear by
   the organization that you think should never be changed?
4. If you were the superintendent, what would you do first?

Hold discussions in a variety of settings: over lunch, coffee,
breakfast, and dinner, with individual parents and parent groups,
elected officials, and businesspeople, in school settings, offsite, or in
corporate or city offices. Search for common themes that resonate
throughout a variety of constituents.

At the end of the ninety days, you should report your findings to
the board. Taking the time to conduct a "listening tour" throughout
your district can help ensure that your suggestions and goals are
well aligned with the board's hopes and expectations for the new

superintendent's performance, as well as with the hopes and expectation of your constituents.

A new superintendent may feel the need to make quick decisions, particularly when the district is in crisis. Research for this study leads to an overwhelming conclusion: Don't. Remember there is a significant difference between acting effectively and acting like you are effective.

If you are hired from within the district, you might feel that you can skip or shorten the time spent meeting with people, listening and learning, since you are already familiar with the inner workings of the district. Listening and learning, however, are well worth your time and attention, regardless of how you arrived in the new role.

The board may have an agenda in mind, but as superintendent you must take the time to make your own assessment before acting. Dr. Sharon Robison, mentor and instructor to superintendents, advises, "When the board is in a hurry, it becomes the role of the superintendent to persuade them to take their time and make carefully planned changes. Until you have become known and trusted in your superintendency, you can't make changes. Don't wield the ax until you have built relationships."

What, then, ought a superintendent do in the first ninety days? Foremost, the goal ought to be meeting with the various constituencies and forming relationships. John Aycock, a former Superintendent of the Year for his region, says, "Shake hands, be genuine, and talk with lots of people. Build relationships. Operate within the concept of keeping the home fires burning with people."

> "By knowing me, community members might be more likely to call me if they had questions or heard something that disturbed them. And, they might be more likely to offer ideas to help create understanding."
> —Johnson et al. (2002, p. 9)

Dr. Wendy Doty, superintendent of over 22,000 students, adds, "Listen to what people are saying. People will lead you in the right direction if you will listen. Ask a lot of questions. Find out what is going on, what motivates people, and what they are upset about."

People generally want the new leader to listen, to hear their concerns, and to act based on what she has learned. "Recognize that you do not have to have the answers," says Dr. Joe Condon, who was recognized as Pepperdine University Superintendent of the Year. "It is OK to have a lot of questions. In fact, it is better."

Superintendents often create an extensive schedule of interviews they plan to hold with members of their community. The purpose of these interactions is to help the leader to better understand the district. "Be visible. Meet with constituents," says Wendy Doty. "Spend the first six months assessing the status of the district. It is exhausting the first year. You don't know what is important and what is not. Only fix what everyone agrees is broken."

> "Visions change, but as the vision evolves, the leader needs to be sure that the 'sacred center'—what everyone holds as paramount—remains intact. That's the first challenge: knowing what the sacred center actually is—from the perspective of others, not just oneself. The second challenge is seeing clearly what must change, even when it is held dear, and getting other people to see it too."—Goleman et al. (2002, pp. 218–19)

Pay especially close attention to the culture of the organization your first few months on the job. "It is a lot of things," says one superintendent, "but mostly it is 'how things get done.' Learn it. It was developed by people who came before you. People tend to reject things that don't work for the culture. Don't go in and mandate how it will get done. Ask. When I first got here, the board said, 'what do you think needs to be done?' I asked for ninety days. I met with over five hundred people. It was a lot of meetings. I came in with a report. I tried to understand what the community and board wanted. I met in homes, in groups, everywhere I could to get the pulse of the community and district."

Hold constant conversations. Conduct informal interviews with students, employees, parents, and community members. Ask how things are going in the district. Use the information you learn to not only connect with people, but also as a guide to better understand the needs of the constituents.

One thing new superintendents should never do is begin their superintendency by acting as though the district began only when they first walked through the door. New leaders might see things they would like to change quickly, but as a rule, superintendents should ignore the instinct to jump in and start changing things.

Sometimes exigent circumstances dictate that there has to be immediate change, but for the most part a leader should simply avoid making major changes in the first few months on the job. If there is no crisis, wait. Don't go in with guns blazing. Never make hurried change before understanding the dynamics and history of the district. Regardless of the pressure you feel to change things or to quickly show people who is in charge and make your mark, the best advice can be summed up simply as "Don't just do something. Stand there."

> "Give the board the time it deserves. Communicate well, value history, value what people are doing. Create a clear direction for where we're going."—Dr. Kent Bechler, superintendent of the tenth-largest school district in California

Remember, it is vitally important to honor those who preceded you and helped to create the district in which you have taken the position. Take the time to meet with people, to learn what is important to them, and to identify the hot topics. Consultation and productive discussions will give you a good feel for what can be changed easily and, more important, what cannot.

The phrase "political capital" can be defined as one's favorable image in the community and among the other important actors inside the district. You should spend political capital wisely. There will be ideas that are honored by the organization, and to immediately attempt to make modifications will expend more political capital than you might earn. People neither expect nor desire immediate change unless a situation is out of control or unsafe. A new superintendent should take her time and pace change efforts as she builds personal, community, and institutional support, banking political capital for when it is most needed.

PROJECT A POSITIVE IMAGE

The expression "Your actions speak so loudly I can't hear what you're saying" is true, particularly in the context of leadership. Most everyone can think of public figures whose image does not engender trust and confidence. Learn from their bad example.

> "Abraham Lincoln said, 'Example is not the main thing in influencing other people; it's the only thing.'"
> —Brady and Woodward (2005, p. 71)

Effective leaders understand that their reflection in the mirror of public scrutiny must show them as they hope to portray themselves to others. Words and actions must be aligned. Instructional educational leaders must reflect a positive image and always remain mindful of how they are perceived. Doing so will inspire and empower the actions of others.

Reflect on how mentoring requires one to consciously set examples for others both on and off the job. Good instructional leaders depict themselves as positive and principled people, whether they are sitting in a wing chair in the boardroom or in the stands at a baseball game.

Effective superintendents don't waver in their respect for others, in their guiding principles and ethics, or in their ability to behave appropriately in a variety of settings. Leaders are the public face of the organization. They know people are constantly learning from, and to some extent mimicking, the leader's behaviors. Take steps to ensure that the examples you set are impeccable. Have fun, but not at the expense of others. A good leader would never risk jeopardizing his career by acting in a way that would reflect poorly on himself or his organization.

Effective leaders influence their team through well-thought-out action. When the superintendent of a large urban district cares enough about classrooms to be out visiting them, principals are quick to realize that they too should be observing in classrooms. Inevitably word quickly spreads that this superintendent places her priority where it should be: in the school.

Discussion Scenario #1: Too Busy

Sally Matthews prided herself on being busy. As superintendent, she always felt most effective when she had just a little more to do than could be done. As a result, Sally was always running just a little bit late. "That shows just how busy I am," she thought to herself. "After all, I'm the superintendent. I think that's how I'm supposed to be."

Sally's colleagues were busy too, and they did not appreciate her constant late arrivals. She would burst in to meetings five to fifteen minutes late, looking harried and hurrying in the door. "Sorry I'm late," she would say. "It's just that I have so much to do today." This behavior was so predictable that Sally's colleagues had begun to place bets on how late Sally would be, and what her excuse would be today.

"I wonder if she thinks the rest of us don't have other things to do," they would mutter.

"I drove all the way over here to meet with her, and I have a busy schedule too," said one of her peers. "I was on time, but this meeting is in her office and she still arrives late. This is starting to bug me."

No sooner would the meetings begin, but Sally's cell phone would ring. "This will just take a minute," she would tell the group. And out the door she would go. Five minutes later she would hurry in the door. "Darn board members are always calling, expecting me to drop everything," she would say.

"That's because you do drop everything," thought one of her colleagues. "Board members are to be respected, but they will understand if she doesn't take their calls when she's in meetings," one muttered to another.

"Now, where were we?" Sally would ask when she returned some minutes later, apparently unaware that her interruptions had irked her colleagues.

"We were discussing time management strategies," said Sarah Wheeler. "This is something we all would benefit from hearing, so it would be great if you would hang in here with us while we work through this item."

Sally's phone rang again. "Oh, gotta get that," she said. Then out the door she went.

(continued)

Discussion Questions

- What impression is Sally making on her colleagues?
- What should Sally's colleagues do in this situation?
- What can Sally do to create a change in her approach to her work?

It may seem counterintuitive that this approach would be effective, or even possible, in a larger district, but that is not the case.

"Value your listening and reading time at roughly ten times your talking time. This will assure that you are on a course of continuous learning and self improvement."—Gerald McGinnis (quoted in Maxwell 1999, p. 21)

Study responses indicated that the larger the district, the more emphatic top superintendents were about the importance of site-level visibility. Large-district superintendents indicated they understood how easy it is to get pulled away from contact with their school sites. Effective instructional leaders make specific efforts to be approachable.

Instructional leadership should be one of the superintendent's main areas of focus. If a superintendent wants teachers and principals to embrace an innovation, that superindendent must demonstrate interest and support by attending training with the staff. When possible, superintendents should attend staff development sessions, be attentive, and remain at events until their conclusion.

Think of the last training you attended. If your boss was there, you probably remember when she arrived at the training, when she left, and how attentive she was throughout the presentation. A superintendent must remember that as the leader, his presence is critical to the success of the activity. The mere act of being there and paying attention shows staff that the training is worth the leader's time, and it is therefore also worthy of theirs.

EXHIBIT STRENGTH OF CHARACTER

Superintendents must quickly learn to develop a thick skin and to become seemingly impervious to personal attacks. A majority of a superintendent's power is derived by the perceived authority the position inherently holds.

When people are upset and ask to speak to the superintendent, much of the time it is not the leader with whom they are angry. Instead, they are often merely seeking to be heard. People want to see whoever is in charge. If you do not seek out the problems in your district, you can rest assured the problems will find you. "You have to feel comfortable with controversy," advises one superintendent. "Don't avoid it."

> "Gather your courage, and if you don't have it, get it fast!"—Dr. Gwen Gross, author and superintendent

The work of the superintendent, both the highlights and the difficult times, will be featured regularly in the paper. Superintendents must become accustomed to this type of regular public scrutiny. As a superintendent, you will doubtlessly face adversity, and you must be prepared to embrace it. Dr. Sharon Robison describes "above the fold" leadership as the day the superintendent's picture appears on the front page, above the fold of the newspaper. When this happens, as it inevitably will to every leader, you can safely assume their day will probably not be a good one.

> "Some time in his or her career, every superintendent faces the 'long walk to the morning newspaper' no matter how long the driveway actually is."—Johnson et al. (2002, p. 27)

IMPROVE YOURSELF

Dr. Dennis Fox, instructional coach, consultant, and specialist, reminds leaders that in order for things to improve in schools, the adults in the organization must continuously get better at what they do. Excellent leaders inculcate this thought into their every action. They attend classes, read voraciously, observe others, seek one-on-one coaching, and participate in learning groups. They understand that no person comes to the job of superintendent with all the knowledge needed for their work. The superintendent's job will inevitably continue to evolve, regardless of whether the leader wants it to. You must be prepared to evolve with it.

Good leaders never stop enhancing their skill sets. Dr. Jean Fuller, a former superintendent of a large district and current California state assemblywoman, described what she terms the "parent phase" as a new administrator, when new administrators are focused on tasks and on doing things in their own way.

> "Once leaders commit to doing the deeply personal work of cutting through the layers of ego, they begin to clarify how to make an authentic contribution in all of their spheres of influence."—Cashman (1998, p. 44)

"In my early days," said Fuller, "task meant something to me. Early in my career task mattered. The longer I was in it, I looked at it differently. It is like a young parent, a middle-aged parent, and a grandparent. You begin with diapers and bottles, the immediate urgency for survival. Then I became a middle-aged parent. 'I'll sit beside you; you drive.'"

The middle-aged parent phase, explained Fuller, is when one focuses on "leadership. Your own ethical background really matters. You focus more on relationship and less on task. You mentor." Over time, Fuller entered what she called the "grandparent phase," the stage when one's focus moves to other people. "You are thinking of others. You're trying to envision next steps for them." By this time, Dr. Fuller explained, a superintendent's work is no longer about completing tasks. An effective leader must now begin to forge relationships and become an agent of change within the school system.

Some districts are dysfunctional, and new leaders may begin to think every district functions as poorly as theirs does. Superintendent peer and networking groups are valuable events at which a new superintendent has the opportunity to "reality test."

It is imperative for new superintendents to meet and interact with their colleagues. Superintendents' groups meet to allow leaders to learn and gain insight by comparing their experiences with those of their counterparts. Interacting with one's peers allows one to ascertain different approaches to common problems. These professional and social groups facilitate discussions about techniques and tactics that work and about ones that don't, and they allow colleagues to discover best practices in the field.

The universe of people with whom a superintendent must meet is much larger than most new leaders will likely ever have experienced. A superintendent's professional network will eventually come to include city, county, and state officials, local merchants, realtors, parents, and other superintendents. John Aycock says, "Don't come in with the expectation that your job is just to fit in to the inner workings and only work inside the district. If you do that, you won't build the network you need."

Another indispensable benefit of building a network of colleagues is that they can help a new superintendent define his responsibilities and tasks, align them with those of others in the field, and gain a better overall perspective of what it means to be a superintendent.

With any luck, there will already be a cohesive working group of superintendents in your area. If there isn't, a good district leader should take the initiative and make connections with other districts. You can begin by contacting neighboring superintendents and starting a networking group that members can call on for advice and questions. Trusted colleagues can make all the difference.

"Treat everything seriously, but don't take anything personally. That wastes so much time. You're going to make decisions day in and day out that make people mad. When you do the right thing, you usually make everybody mad. Develop some comfort with this."—Dr. James B. Phares, AASA Superintendent of the Year National Finalist, 2008

Dr. Wendy Doty suggests, "Pick someone you can talk to a lot. Bounce things off of them. Read books together. Have lunch. Talk with one another about your work. Even when there are large differences in district size, you will quickly find common themes emerging that provide the opportunity for sharing among colleagues."

CONCLUSION

The first year of any job is exciting, but as a new superintendent, it is also important to remember that the first ninety days are a time to proceed with caution. Listen carefully, learn the culture, understand the history, and seek to decipher the desires of the board and constituents. Learn from those who have done this work prior to your arrival. Build a network of peers, and learn from them. Taking the time to be both a learner and a leader is critical to the success of the instructional leader, as well as to that of the organization.

POINTERS FOR NEW SUPERINTENDENTS

(from Dr. Bill Mathis, AASA National Finalist 2003, Vermont Superintendent of the Year, 2003)

- Never take one side of the story, and remember, different people have different spins on the ball.
- Look after money and personnel. Those are the two areas where one is most apt to get into trouble.
- Auditors are your friends. Keep those people close. One can't watch everything. Have natural checks and balances that make sure you have integrity in your operations.
- Get distance between the problem and yourself. Avoid immediate reactions. Take a deep breath. Very few problems can't wait until tomorrow.

IMPLICATIONS FOR ACTION

- Regardless of their training, background, and experience, most superintendents feel underprepared when they begin. In many ways, the work of the superintendent requires initial and ongoing on-the-job training.

- Consider the timing of your first job as superintendent. Don't be in a hurry. Many current and former superintendents advise a late career move to the position.
- Develop a plan for your first ninety days that includes a great deal of listening and learning.
- Don't begin making changes as soon as you assume the role of superintendent. Take the time to learn and understand as much information as possible about the culture, the history of the organization, the wishes of the board, and the needs of the constituents.
- Develop a thick skin. Don't take things personally.
- Be courageous.
- Align words and actions. People look to the superintendent for behavior to model.
- Be a positive influence for others, both on and off the job.
- Lead by example. Attend training and stay until its conclusion.
- Recognize that nobody is expected to have all the answers. Ask questions.
- Develop a network both within and outside the school district. Get out and meet community leaders, state and local political representatives, and local business people.
- Find other superintendents who are willing to mentor you in your early years in your position.
- Pace yourself. "This job is a marathon, not a sprint" (Dr. Jack Gyves).

2

COMMUNICATING LEADERSHIP CHARACTERISTICS THAT BUILD TRUST

EFFECTIVE COMMUNICATION

It has been said, "People don't care how much you know until they know how much you care." One can create a leadership style that builds trust by exhibiting characteristics of effective leadership: communication, strong relationships, service, visibility, and courage. Effective educational leaders know that in order to build effective instructional leadership they must begin by earning the trust of their constituents. Each element of the constituency must feel the superintendent has concern for the team and the students and is heavily invested in creating a positive outcome.

> "The mark of an exceptional leader is in their ability to communicate vision into action."—Dr. Darline Robles, superintendent, Los Angeles County Office of Education

Every district will create unique challenges for its administrator. Some challenges are driven by location, or by the board, or by the temporality and events that drive decision making. Effectively imparting clear guidance to the team can make the difference between meeting a target and falling far short.

The trait of effective communication, above all others, is a leader's most important skill. Words and anecdotes, behaviors including nonverbal and symbolic communication, and actions such as mentoring and serving others all demonstrate the connection between the leader and the staff, the board, and the community at large. One commonality among successful leaders is that each builds a communication hub powerful enough to set the direction for progress.

Developing strong communication skills makes it possible for leaders to carry out the role most central to their work: building an effective instructional system that continuously improves instruction for students. Effective leaders focus their energies on communication to motivate others toward positive change for children. "Effective leaders bring others along with them, mentor, nurture, and empower. They draw people into the effort, helping others to understand they are part of the solution," says Dr. Darline Robles.

A leader must communicate well and connect effectively with people. This critical work is carried out everywhere, even in the classroom. When observing a class, the leader takes very little direct action, but she shoulders ultimate responsibility. Therefore, a superintendent must teach, mentor, train, encourage, and empower others to carry the leader's message to the classroom level.

A leader's ability to communicate well enough that the message penetrates throughout the school system requires building powerful relationships and developing the tools for effective communication. As Dr. Darline Robles says, "There is not any one style. Leaders are not necessarily charismatic. They connect well, they are passionate, and they engage people. They create excitement behind their vision. They are constant and courageous. They change the culture."

"When a leader reaches out in passion, he is usually met with an answering passion."—Maxwell (1999, p. 81)

People not only need to understand the leader's message, but they also must believe that the leader is passionately responding to their needs and desires. Instilling confidence in employees at all levels in the organization requires communication skills that surpass the conventional. The most effective leaders seem to have an uncanny innate ability to get their messages across in positive ways, to recruit people to the cause, and to build strong and effective teams through positive communication.

Developing communication skills can spell the difference between a leader's success and failure. It is solely up to the instructional leader to articulate her most important goal. Strong and effective communication gives action to the collective vision of student success. It is incumbent upon the leader to help workers throughout the district understand they are each a part of the force that fulfills the mission and drives improvements for students.

There are multiple ways for an instructional superintendent to stay in touch with colleagues, constituents, and the community. One of the more recent innovations adopted by successful instructional leaders is creating both a district website and a superintendent's weblog, or "blog." A blog contains regular entries of commentary, descriptions of events, or other material such as graphics or video. "Blog" can also be used as a verb, meaning to maintain or add content to a blog. A typical blog combines text, images, and links to other blogs, web pages, and other media related to its topic.

The most effective websites and superintendent blogs possess three common characteristics:

1. Fresh content
2. Photos that describe or illustrate the story and that are of people other than the superintendent
3. A weekly report of district news

In order to interest readers in visiting the page more than once, it is important to post fresh content that will capture viewer interest, using such "angles" as human-interest stories, an informative article, or a commendation for a job well done. The most effective blogs are freshened with new content at least once each week, along with a photo that illustrates the blog entry.

Some superintendents encourage use of the interactive aspects of the Internet posting by permitting readers to post responses to the blog. While this does encourage a free exchange of ideas, a superintendent might do well to remember that monitoring the content might unduly burden a district's already time-crunched technology staff. While there is something to be said for a blog that contains an interactive component, one ought to be very cautious in implementing such a system. Not everyone is going to respond politely, and some readers may try to use an open blog as a forum for public debate.

Another handy tool instructional leaders can implement on the district website is a weekly Superintendent's Report. One can align the nonconfidential information given to the board in their weekly report with the published public report, which saves time and effort. Posting a weekly report online allows parents, staff, and community members to stay continuously "in the loop" and demonstrates an instructional superintendent's commitment to keeping them informed of current events and opportunities.

Most superintendents use e-mail daily. It can be a quick and efficient method to communicate with people. But at the same time one must always remain cognizant that the hundreds of e-mails a superintendent can receive each day can quickly become overwhelming. Some might find it helpful to manage e-mail by setting aside a specific time each day (say, from 11:30 to noon) to read and respond to e-mails.

One top superintendent describes how he approaches his daily e-mail: "I scan them all, and either respond immediately, file for later reading, or delete them. I answer those that require immediate attention, dropping non-urgent newsletter-style e-mails into files labeled things like 'Read Me,' and delete spam (junk). I refer to the 'Read Me' file when I have time to read informational, informative, or entertaining items that do not require action. I think of this file as my electronic version of that stack of magazines and articles I keep on my nightstand."

A good rule of thumb is that the subject line of an e-mail should be as long as necessary to allow the reader to surmise the content. It shows respect for the reader to let them know the substance of your note without having to read the entire missive. Consider using subject lines that begin with a short descriptor, such as "URGENT," "FYI," or "CONFIDENTIAL." Conversely, e-mail with subject lines such as "Hi" or "Quick Note," or which are rather obtuse and require recipients to peruse the e-mail in order to understand the meaning of the subject line, often irritate the reader.

The very aspect that makes e-mail so appealing, the ability to respond quickly, causes electronic correspondence to be fraught with peril. When e-mails are of an urgent or critical nature, a superintendent, as a leader, must think carefully about how best to respond.

E-mail does not always give the recipient an accurate sense of the message the sender wishes to communicate. E-mail can convey unintended or negative messages because the subtle and often vital nuances of tone and inflection are missing. Sometimes it may be far more beneficial to simply call the sender or schedule a conversation to discuss the content. The spoken word can sometimes ease a tense or difficult situation that might only be exacerbated by electronic communication.

To become more effective communicators, instructional school administrators must also master another aspect of interpersonal communication, "The Art of the Uncomfortable Conversation." In this context, an "uncomfortable conversation" is something important that must

> "Would you prefer limping, or are you ready to remove the stone in your shoe?"—Scott (2002, p. 145)

be said to another person that is likely to make both you and the other party uneasy or discomfited.

How does one begin a conversation that is almost sure to be uncomfortable? Dr. Krista Parent, AASA 2007 National Superintendent of the Year, advises, "It helps to build up chips in your bank account with people, so when it comes time to have the difficult conversation, you already have an established relationship."

It is often hard to know how to proceed when the circumstances indicate that an uncomfortable conversation is in order. The best advice may be that if you cannot say something nice, simply be honest and direct. "I have to tell myself it is my responsibility to have this conversation; it is not my responsibility how they choose to respond to it," remarks Dr. Bill Mathis, AASA Superintendent of the Year for the State of Vermont. He continues, "My moral responsibility remains the same. There will be differences. Some will break down, some will threaten. Some will thank me. It runs the gamut from the dignified to the very undignified."

"The only way you can have an uncomfortable conversation is to just do it," comments Dr. Bill Mathis. "The more direct you are when you speak, the better. There is no getting around the necessity of speaking bluntly. It doesn't mean you have to be tactless or crude." Commenting with a chuckle, Mathis added, "All of these lessons are learned with a little scar tissue."

There are several steps in mastering the art of the uncomfortable conversation. It may not be easy for either you or the other person, but the most respectful way to treat an employee is to be clear about expectations for their performance or about the situation at hand.

First, you must be sure to have a strategy to begin the discussion, as well as an exit strategy with which to end it. Prior to initiating an uncomfortable conversation, you should ask yourself if there is enough evidence to support the concern—is it a big enough issue to discuss in person, vis-à-vis the likely negative impact it will have on your relationships in the district?

Second, think through the content of what you want to communicate. You might wish to jot down key words or phrases about the points you plan to make. Do not make extensive notes, or it is likely you will spend most of your time reading or looking down at your notes and away from the other person. Remember, however uncomfortable, the purpose of the conversation is to engage in dialogue, not to conduct a monologue. A list of bullet points is more than adequate for this type of conversation.

When the time is right, invite the other party, and if appropriate, tell them ahead of time the topic of discussion. Surprising someone with an uncomfortable conversation is generally ill advised. You might find it helpful to caution the other party that they should not anticipate an easy meeting. Instead, without holding the conversation itself, communicate the nature of the meeting and mention that if the other wishes, he may have a representative present. Disciplinary meetings should be arranged in writing. Other meetings might be scheduled verbally. Regardless, the other parties should be informed of your intent to provide them feedback that they may find difficult to hear.

When he plans to have an uncomfortable conversation with one of his subordinates, Dr. James Phares says, "I like to warn them, 'These are serious allegations. What is coming is going to be difficult.'"

Say what you have to say with kindness, but be forthright and honest. One superintendent explains, "I say, 'I have something difficult to talk with you about. This will hurt me as much as it hurts you.' Then I go back to my core beliefs. 'Here's what I've seen and heard. I'm going to be honest with you.' There is coaching involved."

Uncomfortable conversations often create high emotion. Often the reaction of the other party is simply to flee. Understand and allow for this. However, if they wish, and if it is appropriate, let the other person respond, and then end the meeting. Do not mix other business into the discussion, even if the other person or that person's representative attempts to continue.

Finally, it is important to follow up in order to monitor the person's progress in modifying the unacceptable behavior. If the behavior has not been corrected, the instructional leader should restate the original point, being sure to follow it up in writing. Follow the rule of ABC: Always Be Clear. People usually need to process the content of an uncomfortable conversation. Check back with the person within a few days to assess their reaction and to answer any questions they might have.

"Coach people out of the profession if it is clear they are trying to be successful and it's clear it's not going to happen," says Dr. Krista Parent.

> "It is only with the heart that one can see rightly; what is essential is invisible to the eye."—Antoine de Saint-Exupéry, *The Little Prince*

Superintendents must exhibit caring and concern if they wish to be considered outstanding members of the profession. By virtue of empathy as well as occupation, a leader often discovers herself in a position to gain the trust and confidence of her constituents. People open up in ways they might not otherwise, because they believe the leader will keep their issues secret. As people see their secrets are kept, individuals become even more willing to share confidences, and a cycle of trust is built.

At times, the most effective way to communicate is by not talking. Knowing when to keep still is an essential element of effective communication. School superintendents are privy to a great deal of confidential information. It takes only a careless word or an unguarded moment to undo months, or even years, of building trust. There are legal as well as personal repercussions if privileged information is disclosed in the wrong setting or to a person or agency not permitted to receive it. Personal information about employees or private student issues and situations, for example, must not be disclosed except in specific and limited instances as defined by federal and state law.

It is a normal consequence of establishing strong relationships and personal bonds that district leaders may be told or otherwise learn of confidential information. One superintendent says, "I try to spend personal time with people. This may lead to knowing more about people than would normally be within the scope of my role. You must be confidential. You cannot talk about these things outside that setting. Just be quiet, listen, and observe."

> "The best kind of listening comes not from technique but from being genuinely interested in what really matters to the other person. Listening is much more than patiently hearing people out."—McEwan (2003, p. 8, quoted from Richard Farson, *Management of the Absurd: Paradoxes and Leadership*, Simon & Schuster, 1966)

Sometimes knowing when to be quiet does not involve disclosure of personal issues, but instead issues arising in the course of a superintendent's normal work. For example, in the case of a closed-session meeting with the school board, the items discussed therein must remain confidential.

Because of Open Meetings Act requirements, even those who were in the board meeting room cannot discuss closed-session items freely after a closed session is adjourned. For a superintendent to do so is not only a breach of confidentiality, but also a violation of the act. Violating the Open Meetings Act can have myriad repercussions, including leaving the district open to a possible lawsuit, giving away the district's position during a negotiation, or simply shaking the board's faith in its leader. Regardless of the situation, it is imperative that closed-session information always be kept confidential.

Leaders must gauge their actions as well as their words when confidential topics arise. It is a fact that some people are better than others when it comes to masking emotions, which is how outstanding poker players make a living. For district superintendents, it is not uncommon for people to joke about how a particular leader holds

> "While no single conversation is guaranteed to transform a company, a relationship, or a life, any single conversation can."—Scott (2002, p. xv)

his jaw or furrows her brow when attempting to avoid certain topics. Close staff members learn to read a leader's expressions and body language, and though the superintendent at times may not speak with words, actions can speak volumes.

The eyes may be windows into the soul, but one's physiognomic reactions may give the world an unexpected peek into one's heart. It is important that the effective instructional leader learn when and how to apply what has been referred to as "the board benign face." "Board benign" is a carefully crafted facial expression designed to evince concern and empathy while at the same time indicating neither approval nor disapproval.

Individuals are a composite of their life experiences. Practically every person has worked for or known someone who repeatedly said, "Where I worked before, we used to do it this way."

> "Respect the past. Speak the present." —Dr. Louise Taylor

Looking back to another time and place, or to the way things were done someplace else, can sometimes be instructive, and it is natural to seek to apply past lessons to present circumstance. However, constant references to previous positions, districts, or co-workers are often perceived as unnecessary, annoying, inapplicable, inappropriate, or illogical.

When a leader is new to a district, the importance of experience cannot be underestimated. However, it is equally important to lead the team toward new goals by respecting the past while speaking about the present and future. If one waxes nostalgic a bit too often, listeners might wonder, "If you liked it so much where you were before, then why did you leave?"

Experienced leaders should be mindful not to refer to "the way we've always done it around here." The role of the superintendent has almost everything to do with what is and can be, and very little to do with what was. Effective instructional leaders envision the future, build teams, and act as agents for positive change. Past events have brought the district to where it is, but only forward thinking will point the district toward the direction in which it ought to go. Effective leaders think and speak with an orientation to the future.

BUILDING STRONG RELATIONSHIPS

Administrators sometimes complain about interruptions. Sentiments akin to "Wouldn't it be nice if the public would go away so I could actually get my *work* done" are not a rarity. Thinking thoughts like these belie ignorance of a fundamental point: paperwork is a part of the job, but it is merely indicative of the leader's position in the organization. A superintendent's raison d'être is talking with, and listening to, people. When one ascribes greater importance to the paperwork on one's desk than to the people with and for whom one works, one is rather obviously missing the opportunity to build bridges and increase effectiveness.

> "Great leaders engage people in the job and help them to get there."
> —Dr. Darline Robles

"My day is people all day. My paperwork is done after hours," comments Sherry Smith. This approach makes for a very long day, but it also illustrates a central fact. The real work of the superintendent is simply not accomplished by pushing paper; it is accomplished only through effective interaction and communication with the board as well as with parents, staff, students, and the community.

Successful communicators do their most effective work in person. A phone call may get the job done, but a face-to-face discussion will accomplish the task *and* possibly enhance the interpersonal relationship. A strong and reliable network of contacts is indispensable in enlisting the help of others in moving projects and people toward a common goal. It is always more difficult to say "no" to someone with whom one has personally interacted than to another person one knows only as an entry on a mailing list.

Sandra Thorstenson, 2008 Association of California School Administrators Superintendent of the Year for her region, uses this approach: "I have one-on-one conversations when I need to really reach people. I believe in personal engagement. People are blown away by this. They can't believe I'm working so hard to connect with them." Thorstenson says this type of personal attention helps her to quickly identify problems in her district. "Whenever I have an idea I need to sell, I go out and talk with people and gather support and opinions. In talking with people we may take a different path, but the goal likely remains the same."

Similarly, when Dr. Jean Fuller wants to be sure she has built a connection, she says she asks herself, "Did I talk to everyone until I saw their eyes understand? Their eyes show me their heart. I need to get past the emotional screen to intellect. I have to sit with them."

Besides helping to frame future interactions and build relationships, good listening skills provide a wealth of information. "Do a lot of listening," advises former Superintendent of the Year for his region, Manny Barbara. "Keep your ear to the ground so you know what's going on. Listen to people complain. When people do this, it is a chance to obtain information. Don't get too defensive. Be ready to hear everything, including the negative."

The most effective leaders consistently hone their listening skills. John Beck, a fourteen-year veteran superintendent, adds, "If you don't want the answer, don't ask the question." Adds Thorstenson, "If they know you are listening with an open heart, and the plans

Discussion Scenario #2: Floor Plan

It was long the goal of Superintendent Sherelle Jones and the board of trustees to use their facilities funding budget to replace carpets and flooring in several schools. Promises were made to the teachers, who went away for the summer looking forward to starting the next academic year with new floor coverings in their classrooms. Carpet tiles were not even cleaned, because it was anticipated that a change in furnishings was on the way.

In early August, the superintendent received an unexpected call. "I hate to tell you this, Dr. Jones, but the flooring we ordered is not going to arrive on time."

"Teachers can't come set up their classrooms until after it is installed. Precisely when do you estimate that will be?" demanded Jones.

"I'm guessing that will be Sunday afternoon the twenty-first."

"You're telling me that teachers won't be able to set up for the start of school until the afternoon before it starts? We'll need another plan," Jones answered, although perhaps in a more clipped tone than she would have preferred.

The superintendent called the affected principals to discuss the impact of the situation. The discussions yielded few options. The district could wait until the holiday break in December to install the flooring, but that would force teachers to re-create their classrooms midyear. They could skip redoing the flooring until the next year, but the existing carpet had not been cleaned, and they knew that parents as well as faculty would find this objectionable. Or, instead of postponing the renovation, they could instead attempt to schedule installation of the carpet as soon as practicable.

That afternoon, the superintendent spoke with the facilities director. "I need you to find a way to get that carpet in faster. Our teachers have to have the time to set up their classrooms, and we promised them that we would replace their carpets. We can get the carpet faster if we drive to the manufacturer to pick it up, so that's what we'll have to do to make this happen on time."

"Good," said the facilities director. "Let's do it."

Teachers were told in advance that there would be a tighter than normal period for room setup. They were asked if they would need additional help, and aides were scheduled in the days prior to the start of school to help teachers set up. Most significant to the teachers, however, was the fact that their principals and the superintendent were on-site throughout the project, ensuring the flooring was installed as quickly as possible, and that the needs of the teachers were met.

Discussion Questions

- Do you believe Superintendent Jones made the best choice? Why or why not?
- Why did the superintendent choose to be at the school site during this stressful time?
- Do you think this type of leadership would work in your educational setting? Why or why not?

reflect their opinions, they'll be open to them. If you can't reflect their opinions, you tell them so they know why their opinion does not show up in the end product."

SERVICE

There seems to be a uniquely human need to affix blame for a bad decision, an unanticipated action, or an undesired result. Sometimes an effective superintendent comes to the realization she has no choice other than to "take one for the team." The best leaders step up to absorb jabs and punches before they can be thrown at other administrators in their district. By deflecting the blow, a superintendent can ensure the district will continue to function optimally as he or she goes about the business of quietly determining what happened, who is responsible, and how to solve the problem.

> "Sometimes the person people need to be able to blame is you."
> —Anonymous superintendent

"Don't stand alone in the spotlight," says one superintendent. "You should be in the shadows unless the public is critical. In that case, step up." Another superintendent advises, "Some decisions you just have to make. You take the bullet for someone else. Sometimes hard decisions, like boundary changes or school principal transfers, need to be made, and it is the superintendent's job to take that bullet."

Why would anyone put himself or herself in a position to absorb undeserved blame? To paraphrase the plaque on Harry Truman's desk, the buck stops with you. If the superintendent fails to take responsibility for a problem in the district, the effects are likely to ripple directly to the school board; and the board is the group the superintendent is employed to protect.

One superintendent responded to this book's leadership study by relating that she had inherited a small school district in the midst of stormy economic times. Major budget cuts had to be made to avoid turning a catastrophic financial crisis into a complete meltdown. After much discussion, the difficult decision was made to close a school. This, in turn, required boundary changes. School board members heard the words "Don't close our school" from neighbors and friends everywhere they went—at the grocery store, at the gas station, and even while attending their places of worship.

Each school in the district lobbied to remain open. Angry people filled board meetings. The only way the superintendent could keep the district functioning was to take responsibility for the school closure and the boundary change. Though it was not the new leader's "fault," the school had to be closed. By stepping up and taking the blame, the superintendent earned the appreciation and cooperation of the board throughout the rest of her time there.

Effective leaders build strong and dedicated relationships by first serving others. They rise through the ranks in part because they exhibit "servant leadership"—a management style that is defined as being attuned to serving the needs of others.

Typified by selflessness, humility, focus, and commitment to service, servant leadership is an integral personal trait common to the best educational leaders. This service-oriented leader is the kind

Discussion Scenario #3: Declining Dollars

The district had been declining in enrollment for over five years when Sarah Wheeler was hired as the new superintendent. Her predecessor had been fired due to financial mismanagement, and the district was facing catastrophic fiscal issues. Although she knew that new leaders should theoretically not come in and make immediate changes, Superintendent Wheeler felt she had no other choice.

"We must cut one million dollars from our annual budget this year in order to remain solvent," she told the school board.

"We'll need to keep cuts as far away from the classroom as possible," answered the board president.

"Doubtlessly," replied Superintendent Wheeler. "But with a twenty-five-million-dollar budget, one million is going to be a huge cut. Unfortunately, it will impact almost all of our programs. Every year our enrollment declined, our funding was also reduced. But there have been no cuts at all during the last five years. Now the problem is enormous."

"Can't we just get a loan?" one board member inquired.

"If we were to borrow, how would we pay the money back?" asked Superintendent Wheeler. "And who would even think of loaning the district money after they took a look at our financial statements?"

Having no other choice, the governance team gathered suggestions from principals, teachers, classified employees, parents, and community members, and it was finally determined that there was no choice but to lay off a large number of classified employees.

"Oh, this is going to be painful," a school board member lamented. "These employees have worked for us for years. They are members of our community, and this is their livelihood. I didn't join a school board to do this sort of thing!"

Superintendent Wheeler knew she could have delegated the task, assigned it to an assistant, or sent the message by letter. But she did not do any of those things. Instead, she scheduled a one-on-one meeting with every classified employee on the layoff list.

(continued)

When the time came to inform the classified employees of their pending layoffs, she spoke frankly with each person about the district's fiscal situation and about the rationale for their release. She listened respectfully, and she offered to help as best she could in their search for employment. As could be expected, no employee was happy to receive a termination notice. But they were grateful to Sarah for taking the time to meet with them personally and for speaking with them honestly.

Discussion Questions

- Why did Sarah choose to be the one to deliver the news?
- What difference did it make to the employees who left?
- What difference did it make to the employees who remained?

who is most often seen rolling up her sleeves and doing what it takes to meet the needs of her constituents.

There are many examples of servant leadership in the field of education. These leaders walk in the shoes of their staff members, serve their communities, and find appropriate ways and times to recognize others. Effective leaders put others first. When they are acknowledged for doing something great, outstanding leaders thank others first, because they truly believe it was the work of the team that made their individual success possible.

Servant leadership is about putting others first, and in so doing, demonstrating their im-

"There was once a leader of a major monastery in China who was known for his purposeful teaching. However, instead of lecturing people on his teachings and getting lost in theory and concept, he would demonstrate his purposefulness by sweeping the steps of the monastery with all his being. People would come to the entry inquiring about the leader of the monastery, and the 'sweeper' would say, 'The teacher is teaching now.' Since most of the aspirants were focused on looking for something external, 'the teacher,' they rarely recognized that the entire teaching and meaning were present in how the sweeper approached his work life."
—Cashman (1998, p. 65)

portance to the leader and to the organization. Top educational leaders demonstrate their service orientation by putting others first. For example, if a number of people are exiting a meeting at the same time, or queuing up for food during a break, one can exhibit servant leadership merely by encouraging others to go ahead.

Making others feel welcome in work settings is an important way a superintendent can demonstrate commitment to others. An effective leader will not hesitate to walk up to strangers, welcome them with a warm smile and a handshake, and invite them to join a working group. Another example of servant leadership might be a superintendent offering to give up his chair and standing if there is a shortage of chairs at a continuing-education event.

Servant leadership is not a matter of having free time and filling it with community service. Instead, it is a matter of making the time to work within the community. Effective superintendents quickly come to the realization that there is no better time to support and help others than when they lead the team.

> "Being in power is like being a lady. If you have to tell people you are, you aren't."—Margaret Thatcher (quoted in Maxwell 1988, p. 21)

Some of the busiest superintendents in the largest districts demonstrate a keen understanding of the importance of serving others with humility and working hard beside their staff members in order to accomplish commonly held goals. Partnering with staff and the community sets a clear example that service is encouraged and appreciated throughout the organization. Acts of servant leadership such as this will earn the leader gratitude and affection within the community.

VISIBILITY

Visibility is critical to the success of the superintendent, particularly when it comes to visiting school sites. Grounds people do not merely groom a school lawn; they make the school a great setting in which learning takes place. Kitchen workers do not merely serve food; they provide the fuel that helps the students focus on scholarship. Top instructional leaders ought to take time out of every school visit to remind employees that each is an integral part of the team, that every staff worker plays a vital role in building student achievement, and that each person's work makes a difference for students.

Instructional leaders understand the importance of building trust by being conspicuous. Ask a teacher how often she sees her school and district leaders and you will likely hear a comment like "not very often."

In districts with exceptional instructional leaders, site and classroom visits are a part of what the leaders do every week, whether they oversee one site or forty. This visibility is intentional. There is power in visiting a site. These personal calls facilitate one-on-one communication with employees at every level. They palpably demonstrate the leader's interest in the activities at the school and allow them an opportunity to see firsthand the quality of instruction in classrooms throughout the district.

> "His cardinal mistake is that he isolates himself, and allows nobody to see him; and by which he does not know what is going on in the very matter he is dealing with."—Abraham Lincoln, upon relieving General John C. Frémont from his command in Missouri, September 9, 1861 (quoted in Phillips 1992, p. 13)

Site visits allow the leader to, as Dr. Juli Quinn puts it, "stand in the classroom and look back up the system." Leaders can derive immense benefits by visibly conducting field research on how well the district is serving students and teachers and gathering feedback regarding potential improvements. Exemplary instructional leaders understand they cannot function as effective leaders by sitting in an office. They work best by leaving the office and serving their district by communicating constantly with all members of the educational community.

What do effective superintendents do during a site visit? They walk the site with the principal. They make time to look at facilities and discuss maintenance concerns. They make a real effort to visit as many classrooms as possible.

Some superintendents find it beneficial to seek out informal conversations, while others watch classroom instruction. Dr. Sharon Robison suggests, "Swing through the cafeteria. Talk with the custodian. Ask the aides how things are going. Sit down for ten minutes and talk with the principal. A high priority for me was probationary teachers. I would check on each several times per year."

"I visit sites on Fridays," says Dr. David Vierra, an experienced high school district superintendent. "I just walk around and observe. When I visit classrooms, I don't evaluate teachers. I just look to see what the kids are doing. I let the principal know I'm there, and I let them know when I leave. I give a 'heads up' to the principal about what I saw. I give the principals the opportunity for correction if there is a problem. I express any concerns. I make a point to be honest with people."

Dr. Jody Dunlap, former Pepperdine Superintendent of the Year, also takes her leadership team and makes them responsible for soliciting anonymous comments at sites. The comments are compiled and passed along to the site principal for use in planning staff development. Says Dunlap, "When there are hardships regarding instruction, I'll ask teachers, 'What can we as a district do to help you get over this hurdle?'" She adds, "Teachers appreciate this."

Due to the size of his former district, Jim Brown had difficulty visiting every classroom. Instead, he developed a different method of being effective. "I put myself into situations where I could encounter teachers. I would spend time figuring out what in each classroom matters, is tolerated, and is not acceptable. I would get great mileage when I taught a class."

During site visits, effective leaders model the way they want students to be treated. They observe, inquire about student work, and even read stories to younger children. "I remind people that everyone here is some person's child or grandchild, and they are loved," says Dr. Darline Robles.

Leading with one's feet—that is, actually visiting sites and interacting with people—is critical to a superintendent's success. Outstanding district leaders regularly visit sites. Not one respondent to the author's survey considered site visits an onerous task that takes time away from more important things. Top leaders unanimously considered it a vital part of the job. Emphasized one, "It is not an option for me not to visit sites. To me, that IS the work. I want to be sure the teachers know the superintendent appreciates their work."

How often is it appropriate to visit? "I don't think you can be at sites too much," says Sharon Robison. "But don't do drop-ins. Let the principal know when you're going to be visiting school sites."

Superintendents must recognize they have as much to learn from teachers as they have to offer. Taking the pulse of each campus can help district leaders to better understand their effectiveness and perhaps to gain insights into aspects of their message that are not "getting through." Educational leaders do not visit schools to "catch educators in the act of teaching." Instead of visiting for monitoring, successful leaders visit to research and gather information firsthand. They discover the needs of the site, notice things that need fixing, and influence the quality of instruction, as well as things such as the speed of repairs to the facility.

LINCOLN'S PRINCIPLES

- Refrain from reading attacks upon yourself so you will not be provoked.
- Don't be terrified by an excited populace and hindered from speaking your honest sentiments.
- It's not entirely safe to allow a misrepresentation to go uncontradicted.
- Remember that truth is generally the best vindication against slander.
- Do the very best you know how—the very best you can—and keep doing so until the end.
- If you yield to even one false charge, you may open yourself up to other unjust attacks.

- If both factions or neither shall harass you, you will probably be about right. Beware of being assailed by one and praised by the other.
- The probability that you may fall in the struggle ought not to deter you from the support of a cause you believe to be just.

—Quoted in Phillips (1992, p. 75)

COURAGE

Good leaders do not seek out trying circumstances; they instead anticipate problems and attack before they develop into a crisis. They summon the nerve to determine what is right, and act with integrity to resolve the issue promptly and thoroughly.

Exceptional instructional leaders build a framework of trust through the wise application of courageous action. Courage is not necessarily synonymous with charisma, conspicuous heroism, or outspoken bravado. Sometimes the quietest and most thoughtful of people are those who are the most courageous. Courage is not derived from anger or an interest in combat. It is born from self-confidence and principled conviction.

> "Courage is not the absence of fear, but rather the judgment that something else is more important than fear."—Ambrose Redmoon

When district leaders were surveyed about how they handled their most difficult situations, not one of them indicated that they questioned whether they should become involved in a particularly messy or unsettling situation. Instead, they described how they found the courage to address a situation because there was something important to accomplish, a goal to be achieved, or a point to be made. When it was most needed, these leaders were able to set aside their own fears and confront the circumstances. They might not have considered it at the time, but upon reflection, each leader said that on some level he or she innately knew it was time to exhibit courageous leadership.

ANTICIPATE CAUSE AND EFFECT

Good leaders build trust in part merely by preventing bad things from happening. To be an effective leader, one must monitor situations and predict their potential impact. For instance, one should always carefully weigh the benefits gained from intervening against the costs of allowing events to run their course.

Effective superintendents are keen observers and develop a deep understanding of the inner workings of their school district. They flourish when they are aware of the depth of feelings constituents may have. They are attuned to emotional "hot buttons" when contemplating a change. Superintendents thrive by making it a priority to know and understand the desires of the various factions within their organization, tapping in to students, parents, staff, community members, and even local clubs and organizations. No one has a crystal ball, but when leaders take the time to listen to all levels within the organization, they create a higher probability of averting calamity.

Once one becomes aware of a potentially negative situation, as an effective leader it is essential to be completely truthful with one's constituents. As hard as it seems, effective instructional leaders will always choose to face the facts and prepare as best they can for the impending difficulty. If a highly regarded employee needs to be moved out of her present position, a perceptive superintendent will already be sensitized to the likely upset that the transfer will cause. Instead of being caught unaware or being blindsided by the reaction to the situation, the effective leader will instead work through the change process with the concerned party, explaining factually but within legal limits the logic behind the move and salving the wounds as best as possible.

Active listening, telling the truth, and allowing people to voice opinions in opposition to one's own helps to build trust. The public, one's staff, or other constituencies may not get what they want, but in order to allow a leader to continue to guide effectively, these parties must always feel as though they have been heard. Anger is felt with less intensity when people believe someone is listening to

Discussion Scenario #4: The Picnic Debacle

The Jefferson School District was struggling with declining student achievement on the state exam. A team had been convened to study the problem and came up with a list of the ways that district policies impacted instructional time. In one particularly telling illustration, the team concluded that there was too little instructional time spent on task, and that noninstructional assemblies and field trips were interrupting core academic time.

Superintendent Galen Cohen was intensely interested in this issue and sought all the input he could get that he thought might help to fix the system. "Let's start to streamline instruction by taking away all noninstructional field trips and assemblies," suggested Charlotte Carter, the chief business officer. Cohen indicated his agreement with a nod of his head.

A revised policy banning noninstructional assemblies or field trips was soon put into place. Staff and students were disappointed that they would not be able to take noninstructional field trips like the annual outing to the ballpark, but they complied with the new rule nonetheless. It was not until it was time for the end-of-year picnic that things went awry.

As the district's relatively new superintendent, Dr. Cohen was unaware that the picnic was a thirty-year tradition. When the board of trustees heard the cherished event would be canceled, the group became upset.

"What do you mean you canceled the picnic? That picnic is a tradition that goes back to when I went to school. How dare you just demolish our traditions!" exclaimed a senior board member.

"I am merely trying to promote student achievement," replied Dr. Cohen. "You all agreed with the ban on noninstructional trips when we initiated it earlier this year."

The excoriation of the superintendent continued until the meeting mercifully ended. As he drove morosely home, Dr. Cohen was grateful for the chance to be alone at last with his thoughts. "Ugh. What a mess," he groaned as he sped through the dark and moonless city toward home.

(continued)

Discussion Questions

- Who was right in this scenario? Does it matter?
- How could the superintendent have done a better job of gauging cause and effect in this situation?
- What should the superintendent do now?

their concerns. Listening will in turn engender confidence in one as a leader, and grow the trust of the constituents in one's district.

CONCLUSION

It is especially important for effective instructional leaders to strive to become clear communicators. To give and receive information effectively, one must listen actively and speak and write clearly, honestly, appropriately, and openly. Whatever discomfort this may generate initially, a free exchange of ideas will inevitably pay dividends. Subordinates who learn there is no penalty for speaking forthrightly to leaders who are willing and interested in listening can create a powerful, and likely productive, combination.

Instructional leaders can build a strong and lasting foundation of trust with peers, assistants, staff, boards, and throughout the community in a variety of ways. Some of the more effective techniques include ongoing communication, accepting responsibility, and mentoring others. Building professional networks, attending to constituent relationships, and fostering a climate of selfless service are other key components of an instructional leader's success.

Best practices include visibility in the community, becoming aware of, and responding to, the board's interests, demonstrating courage in the face of adversity, being truthful, and remaining cognizant of the ramifications of any decision. The foundation of successful instructional leadership is created by employing a combination of these tactics, not just one. Any positive action a superintendent can take to facilitate trusting relationships will to some degree influence a superintendent's success.

IMPLICATIONS FOR ACTION

- In order to build trust, instructional leaders must become skilled at the art of effective communication.
- The more one develops ability to connect effectively with others, the better one will be able to accomplish the most important work of an instructional leader, that of positively impacting student achievement.
- Accept responsibility: even if one is not responsible for sub-optimal outcomes, effective instructional leaders step up and take responsibility when things go awry.
- Hold uncomfortable conversations, saying what needs to be said clearly and concisely, but with sensitivity.
- Earn trust by keeping nonpublic information in confidence.
- Respect the past, but speak to the present. Focus discussions on what can be, not on the way things were.
- One can build a self-sustaining organization and augment one's legacy by nurturing the skills and abilities of others.
- Understand the importance of the superintendent's physical presence. Visit school sites, and attend school and district functions.
- Demonstrate servant leadership: remember that in order to lead effectively, sometimes one must quietly follow. Become comfortable doing for others and allowing subordinates to be recognized for their positive contributions.
- Conquer fear. One must confront difficult issues despite personal discomfort.
- Effective instructional leaders anticipate events and take positive steps to mitigate potentially negative consequences. Act judiciously in order to create the best possible outcomes.

3

THE GOVERNANCE TEAM

THE ROLE OF THE BOARD AND THE SUPERINTENDENT

There is no group more central to the success of the superintendent than the school board. The board is elected expressly to make decisions on behalf of students, parents, and residents. It represents the voice of the community.

If one were to write a recipe for a typical school board, it might read, "Take a unique blend of different but complementary personalities, motivations, and abilities. Mix in the strong opinions of constituents. Liberally spice with conflict and emotion. Fold in gallons of determination, add an equal measure of enthusiasm and a pinch of politics, and then thoroughly blend."

Unlike a good recipe, there is simply no way to predict the nature (or taste) of an individual school board. Each board has its own unique flavor, which will inevitably develop and change due to factors beyond the superintendent's control: time, election outcomes, and shared experience.

It takes the combined efforts of both an exceptional instructional leader and a strong school board to build an outstanding district. If the superintendent is analogous to the hub of a wheel, then the board is the engine that keeps that wheel turning. With effective steering and skillful control, the governance team can drive the mechanism and the district can go far.

Without that power, a superintendent has very little ability to move the district forward on her own. On strong governance teams, the board members and the superintendent work together. Members and the superintendent alternate leading and following, listening and speaking, and being active or passive. The team keeps off-the-record information confidential, knows when and how to convey essential facts to constituents, and understands the nuances of sensitive issues.

The converse is true of the dysfunctional governance team. Members govern neither themselves nor others well, and the team fails to act as a unit. If either the board or the superintendent is weak, the governance team system is likely to fail, and the important work of the district will not be effectively carried out.

It is perhaps when observing a weak or dysfunctional governance team that one can gain an appreciation for the overwhelming importance of a strong intergroup dynamic. A governance team truly is greater than the sum of its component parts. Smart school boards make a rigorous effort to choose their superintendent well, and wise superintendents remember the importance of maintaining a good relationship with the school board.

> "But you and your board should keep in mind that, no matter how strong your board's partnership with your superintendent might appear at any given time, you cannot afford to take it for granted. Human relationships are always fragile, and this one is no exception; indeed, the forces working against a healthy board-superintendent partnership are daunting."—Eadie (2005, p. 71)

School boards play a key role in guiding the district, and their responsibility includes selecting the superintendent. Board members often say there is no role more central to their work. The selection of a district superintendent is a serious task that ought to be performed with care and diligence. Candidate searches are usually conducted over a period of several months and often involve the use of experienced consultants and recruiters. School boards that make rash decisions or "go it alone" when choosing a superintendent might one day look back and regret their lack of comprehensive planning.

The role of the district superintendent carries with it myriad responsibilities. "The job, as confusing as this may seem," says one superintendent, "is to take a group that is your boss and organize a team to get the job done that they want done."

> "You think the board has chosen you to be the boss, but that's not it. This thinking creates conflict."
> —Anonymous superintendent

The instructional superintendent has numerous duties to fulfill. The superintendent is accountable for forging relationships on behalf of the school board, for determining if facility, environmental, personnel, or systemic changes should be made to create more positive student experiences, and for allocating the human and material resources of the district.

An instructional leader must communicate with the board, faculty, and community. As a multifaceted leader, the superintendent listens and learns about the district, articulates the need for change, creates a vision, and gathers people behind the goal of continuous improvement. He or she works closely with the board to develop common goals, strategies, and tactics that are directed toward fulfilling the expectations of the staff, the hopes of the parents, and ultimately the needs of the students.

The superintendent must spend a tremendous amount of time making sure relationships with and among the governance team are sound and the board is kept informed. No matter the powers assigned to the superintendent, exercising authority depends on the entwined relationships of the governance team. If this group does not mesh well, nothing else in the district will work particularly well. Superintendents are employed by the board, and without the board's full support, an administrator's power is greatly diminished.

Survey responses indicated that some superintendents spend over half their time working with, educating, and building rapport with their school boards. Others said they spend less than 10 percent of their time on board relations. The wide disparity in these figures has to do with many intrinsic and extrinsic factors that can

Discussion Scenario #5: The Preschool Predicament

Dr. Lea Thomas was excited. She was meeting with a group of principals who were strong and capable leaders in her rural school district.

"Things are running pretty smoothly," said one of the principals, "but there are a few things we would like to see happen. Foremost, our students would really benefit from preschool. Because we're in a rural area, they don't have the same options other kids do. Preschool would really give them a leg up."

"We have some funds we can use if we all agree," replied Dr. Thomas. They did, and a team was chosen to formulate a plan for preschool in the district. After months of intense work the team drafted a grand scheme that included how the preschool would operate, who would run it, and when it would begin. One snowy February night, Lea and the principals gathered at the board meeting. She gave a detailed presentation, and after she finished, she thought to herself, "This is a pretty tough board, but we have a great plan here. This had to knock their socks off."

Dr. Thomas was correct. The board's socks were knocked, but not in the way she hoped. Instead, the board reacted with stunned quietude.

"You talk about this preschool as if it was a done deal," said the board president. "But you never once consulted with us. It isn't in our board goals, and to be honest, I think preschoolers are a nuisance. Why would we ever want to bring kids to school any earlier than we have to?"

Another board member made his feelings known rather loudly. "Apparently we need to remind you, Ms. Superintendent, that you work for us. We don't work for you. We determine what is going to happen, and your job is to tell us how you're going to get it done. Perhaps that slipped your mind?"

Now it was Dr. Thomas and the principals' turn to sit in stricken silence. Obviously, this wasn't going to be as easy as any of them hoped.

Discussion Questions

- What did Dr. Thomas do wrong?
- What steps should she have taken? In what order?
- How best might she have averted this situation?

include the demands of each board, the board members' skill levels, the abilities of the superintendent, and the expectations of both the superintendent and the board.

It serves a superintendent well to remember that those who complain about the amount of their time their board requires probably do not really understand that the board is their primary job. A new superintendent may think that focusing on student achievement is the first step toward instituting improvements, but district leaders cannot improve instruction without the buy-in of the school board.

> "Superintendents say, 'If the board would just leave me alone, I could do my job.' But the board is your job."—Anonymous superintendent

The initial step toward achieving any goal is to gain the board's support by earning its trust. Absent that, the entire journey is likely to end in failure.

Superintendents should always speak highly of their constituents in public as well as in private settings. District leaders can be heard from time to time complaining about their boards. At a private party, one superintendent overheard another refer to her board as "just a bunch of bus drivers." Inevitably, those words got back to the board. What that now-former superintendent evidently failed to realize is that the board members were also her bosses.

> "It takes two to do the partnership tango, and at the heart of every really solid board-CEO working relationship . . . is a CEO who is truly . . . board savvy. You will know a board-savvy superintendent by his or her (1) positive attitude toward the board, (2) commitment to playing a leading role in building board governing capacity, and (3) knowledge and expertise in the governing 'business.'"—Eadie (2005, p. 78)

Not only how one acts, but also what one says, and how one says it, carries great weight. It is axiomatic that good news travels fast, but gossip travels even faster. Making nasty, rude, or ill-conceived observations about someone will practically ensure that those words will exhibit the uncanny characteristic of reaching the ears of that individual almost as soon as they are uttered.

Superintendents ought to keep in mind that their remarks are doubtlessly going to be listened to, and they will be repeated to others. It is best to be positive and supportive even in social situations or under adverse circumstances. For instance, it would have been quite helpful for the aforementioned hapless superintendent to remember that though she may not have intended her comment about her board disparagingly, her words perhaps unintentionally also reflected her low opinion of bus drivers ... and her district employed a lot of school bus drivers.

It is the role of the superintendent to set up systems that facilitate effective employee selection at all levels throughout the district. Once a superintendent has been hired, the personnel work of the board ought to be limited to supporting the work of the staff through its approval process, discussing items brought to them from the negotiation table, and paying special attention to personnel issues and items as they are brought to the board's attention by the superintendent.

"The superintendent tells the board who they think is doing well and who they think is not doing well. They come back to the board for support. But it is my decision. I am building my team."—Anonymous superintendent

A superintendent may have board members who want to participate on interview panels. A majority of top administrators discourage this by reminding board members that they are a part of the candidate approval process. Consequently, the board should not also be involved in the selection of those candidates.

Remember: if a superintendent invites board involvement, it is very likely that he will receive it. It is a superintendent's prerogative to keep the board apprised of a situation. Once a leader asks the school board to assist in making personnel recommendations, it should come as no surprise that the board may develop a reasonable belief that this "help" will be requested in the future.

An overwhelming number of superintendents agree that an effective instructional leader should involve many constituencies in the hiring process. Community members, employees, union representatives, parents, even students can play a part. School board members, however, should not participate, because they should not both select and approve candidates. Not only might there be an ostensible conflict of interest, but also the role of the superintendent in guiding the district can be diminished.

If the school board decides to be involved in employment decisions, one of three alternatives is likely to be true. First, board members may be poorly trained and thus cannot be expected to understand their proper role in the hiring and approval process. Second, the board might be micromanaging. Last, and, for a superintendent, worst, a school board asking to be involved in the hiring process might be indicating its lack of faith in the district leader. Regardless of which of these scenarios might be correct, a superintendent needs to reverse the inclination of board members to overstep their roles.

Most people have a set of core values and beliefs, rules by which they choose to live. Most people also carry with them a sense of their personal "bottom line," those issues on which they will not compromise. A leader's bottom line is often found at the

> "The first rule of holes: when you're in one, stop digging."—Columnist Molly Ivins (quoted in Maxwell 1999, p. 44)

juncture where character, values, and moral dilemmas crash into one another.

A leader's bottom line is the point at which she discovers that her mission-critical work meets stiff resistance. This opposition or obstructionism may call for the leader to take a stand. As an example, uninterrupted instructional time might be a superintendent's bottom-line expectation. Challenges to, or conflicts with, that expectation should be met by the superintendent's insistence that academics come first.

Life does not always work as well in practice as it does in theory. Accordingly, district leaders must develop and carry with them what one superintendent refers to as a "floating bottom line." This is not to be confused with an abandonment of personal beliefs and principles. Instead, a floating bottom line indicates a willingness to be flexible in the short term in order to facilitate achieving a longer-term goal.

School boards will not always be as eager to make change as might be a superintendent. Sometimes a leader has no option but to shift his bottom line in order to bring the school board along at a pace at which they are comfortable moving. While this is likely to be frustrating for the superintendent, district leaders must become inured to the notion that theirs is not the final word.

> "Commitment is about a group of intelligent, driven individuals buying into a decision, precisely when they don't naturally agree. In other words, it's the ability to defy a lack of consensus."—Lencioni (2005, p. 51)

Maintaining a floating bottom line can be exasperating. Superintendents know what their personal bottom line would be if they were solely in charge. If the school board's bottom line differs from that of the superintendent, the superintendent must adjust in order to collaborate with the board, not the other way around. If over time it becomes apparent that the superintendent's perspective oftentimes falls on the end of the continuum opposite that of the board's, there is likely an alignment issue. It is incumbent on the superintendent to figure out how to reconcile the differing points of view.

> "When board members hire a new superintendent, they have typically discussed with one another the detailed qualities they desire for their new leader. Members come to consensus on such things as background, education, and experience. Topics not often discussed are the 'other things' that individual board members believe a superintendent should do. These elusive 'other things' sometimes have the greatest impact on the superintendent's relationship with an individual board member or the whole board."—Townsend et al. (2007, p. 13)

Understanding what the board believes is the proper pace of change can be a difficult part of a superintendent's work. A leader may believe it is prudent to make slow and steady progress on a particular issue, while the school board is impatient to effect change. One superintendent says, "I need to tell boards, 'I can make your district better in six months, but you will get lots of pressure to fire me.' The challenge is to get from where we are to where we ought to be without that upheaval."

BUILD A HIGH-PERFORMING GOVERNANCE TEAM

No one who does not already understand the rules of the game is recruited for a college football team. Everyone knows how to play the game and how to play their particular position. There is constant instruction and communication between coaches and players, and there is feedback given at practices, before the game, at the half, and throughout the contest.

When the stakes are high and a game comes down to the final seconds, what does a smart coach do? He rallies his players and huddles with them to discuss amending the game plan to fit the exigencies of the moment. Then he sends his team back onto the field with the tactics to carry out his strategy. Much like a football team, effective school boards also practice and strategize so they too can hit the field ready to execute.

As with any high-functioning team, trust between the school board and the district superintendent is built on clear and strong communication. Every member of the governance team should understand his or her role, and each should be attuned to the interests, strengths, and abilities of the other players. Everyone must recognize the strategy and tactics the team will employ to win. Individual team members might not necessarily agree, but the team must always function as a unit.

Most board members want to be good at their job. As an instructional leader, it is the superintendent's job to help them achieve that goal. One way of teaching new board members about their responsibilities is for a superintendent to take the lead in discussing the time requirements of school board membership during pre-election candidate orientation.

> "There are known knowns. These are things we know that we know. There are known unknowns. That is to say, there are things that we know we don't know. But there are also unknown unknowns. There are things we don't know we don't know."—Donald Rumsfeld

During the session, the superintendent should introduce the candidates to the weighty responsibilities of the office they seek.

Candidates who are running for the school board with ulterior motives, such as a dislike for certain members of the sitting board, or to act as advocates on behalf of the teachers' union, may also discover the real work of a school board is more daunting than they expect. "There is a culture that builds up in running for the board to be a watchdog," says one superintendent.

After listening to a frank discussion of the expectations and challenges of a board position, some candidates might decide not to continue. It is better to lose an aspirant than to have that person elected. When candidates self-select themselves out of the electoral process, it is likely because they feel they would be overwhelmed by the job.

School board members who make a positive impact begin as learners and, over time, develop into leaders. The most effective school board members understand they do not know everything. They come prepared to learn.

The most erudite board members begin their terms with open minds and the understanding that they have a great deal to learn. They willingly attend training, workshops, and conferences, do "outside reading," and attend lectures to learn more about governance. As they gain experience, good board members will mentor newer members. As educators, we know that those who are willing to admit they need to be trained and who listen to what they are taught are often the top students. When board members demonstrate this type of zeal, they contribute to building a solid leadership team that wants to make a positive difference for students.

"Many school boards in the United States fall short of realizing their full governing potential in practice, depriving their districts of sorely needed leadership and their members of the satisfaction that participation in serious governing work can provide. The basic reason for their failure to perform at peak capacity as governing bodies . . . is that these boards are seriously underdeveloped and undermanaged as organizations."—Eadie (2005, p. 5)

Solid team members hold their ground during board meetings both calm and acrimonious. They foster the impression that they are understanding people who listen to their constituents. They keep

Discussion Scenario #6: The Watchdog

At every school board meeting, district superintendent Fred Timms would invariably hear Jack Nelson rip open his sealed packet of background information for the first time.

"Oh, that's just painful," thought the superintendent. "All the time we spend gathering information and compiling those packets, and Jack never opens his until he gets here. He hasn't even seen the agenda until just now. How can he possibly be prepared?"

Jack didn't mind opening his agenda at the last minute. He had been a board member for quite a long time, and he considered it a personal specialty of his that he could "wing it" with little or no preparation. "This board stuff isn't that hard. Why waste time? If I prepare too far ahead I'll forget what I wanted to ask. My best questions come when I see things for the first time."

Jack was proud of his grasp of numbers. When the district budget was an agenda item, he would customarily have plenty of questions. About ten minutes into that evening's budget presentation, he broke in, "On page forty seven, line thirty-two, what is that $95.14 expenditure?"

"There's quite a bit of information in this report," Superintendent Timms said. "It would really have been helpful to have had that question ahead of time."

Nelson puffed up his chest as he said with evident self-pride, "As a board member, I feel responsible to the public to be a watchdog,"

As the district's trusty business official hurriedly flipped through a large stack of backup materials to research the line item, Nelson chided Superintendent Timms: "It appears that you're not especially well-prepared for this meeting."

After what seemed to be an eternity of searching, the business official piped up, "Here it is. The $95.14 you asked about. It is from the board conference, for a meal at the Premier Steak House. The expense was for a prime rib dinner. Yours."

Nelson reddened with embarrassment as he looked at the ceiling, then at the floor, and then back to the ceiling.

(continued)

"You bought the most expensive meal on the backs of the children of our district?" exclaimed the board member seated nearest to Mr. Nelson. Chimed in another, "Jack Nelson! Shame on you!"

"That's not going to be an easy thing for the board or anyone else to digest," thought Superintendent Timms. "Finally, Jack is getting his just desserts."

Discussion Questions

- What can Superintendent Timms do to help Jack Nelson better prepare for meetings?
- What is the role of the board president in attempting to modify Mr. Nelson's behavior?
- What is the best way for the governance team to work together to prevent another incident like this one?

the district's vision and mission uppermost in mind. Boards are often called upon to withstand public scrutiny, cope with labor unrest, or brave the attacks of special-interest groups. A high-functioning school board will develop strategies in advance to meet these challenges while continuing to focus on what is best for students.

COMMUNICATE WITH THE GOVERNANCE TEAM

It is helpful for superintendents striving to become effective instructional leaders to remember that being a member of a school board can often be overwhelming. The board's work frequently is different from any the members have ever been asked to perform. One veteran superintendent says, "It is the prime example of people moving into a job when they don't know what it is."

Training is one of the keys to creating a high-functioning board. Superintendents should do their best to inform prospective or newly elected board members about the job before they take office. Once new board members are in place, the superintendent should make it a mission to teach them how to function most effectively. The school board's responsibility is unique. The simplest way to define the role of the board versus that of the superintendent and staff is that the school board focuses on the "what," the others focus on "how."

Dr. Jack Gyves says that there are three pieces to the puzzle. "'What? (What are we trying to do?), How? (How do we impart these concepts for these children?), Did we? (Did we make our goals?)' In this model, the board is in charge of 'what' and 'did we?' Staff is responsible for 'how' things get done."

Superintendents can help a board grow stronger and perform at a higher level. Spending time with board members and teaching them to deal with controversy more effectively can be helpful in preparing them for the difficult times they will face as members of a school board.

> "It is amazing to me how a group of intelligent, highly educated adults, all of whom speak the same language, can sit in a room for two hours of discussion and then leave the room under the false impression that everyone is on the same page."
> —Lencioni (2005, p. 54)

Working with members to help them master the "board benign face" can be worthwhile. "Board benign" is a controlled facial expression designed to convey a message of caring without betraying other emotions. Effective governance team members will often don board benign faces when listening to individuals haranguing them at board meetings.

Dr. Rene Townsend, co-author of four leadership books, suggests that superintendents develop a comprehensive plan for teaching their boards, saying, "Help the board to understand what it looks like when it is done well."

Many superintendents find it helpful to take the entire school board through yearly boardsmanship training refresher courses. Ongoing training gives members of the board the space and opportunity to redefine their roles by reminding them of the important structures that should exist within the team. Refresher courses in boardsmanship give members the chance to renew their skills. Training can be highly beneficial, particularly when following an election. "Every election you have a new board member, you have to remember you also have a new board," reminds Renee Whitson, former Association of California School Administrators Region XI Superintendent of the Year.

When board members are interested in a collaborative relationship, they will usually agree to ask questions prior to a board meeting so all attendees can arrive prepared. There are board members, however, who will wait until the board meeting to ask detailed questions in order to catch a staff member off guard. If this behavior occurs, it is the role of the superintendent or board president to address the behavior in a diplomatic but corrective way.

A wise superintendent takes advantage of third-party training opportunities whenever possible, because governance training is both important and complex. It is often far more effective for someone else to teach the board the basics of boardsmanship than for the superintendent to do it, because part of the training includes defining the role of the board. Information is often better received from an outside source than from a district leader.

It may appear self-serving for the superintendent to define the board's limited scope of authority by reminding members they do not have the authority to act independently of one another. If this same information is imparted by an outsider, individual board members will likely be more accepting that they cannot operate without consensus.

Absent an outside consultant, the superintendent may have no choice but to assume the role of instructor. It is not always easy for the superintendent to act as an instructional leader for his or her board. Some board members may refuse to attend boardsmanship training, and others might scoff at the notion of paying a consultant to work with them. In cases such as these, the superintendent will likely discover there is a more wide-ranging problem than just a training issue, and this knowledge can help an instructional leader tailor his or her presentation accordingly.

It is the role of the instructional leader to inspire and advise. "One of the basic things you have to communicate with the board is to tell them what you want," says one superintendent. It behooves the superintendent to remember that the final decision on any issue, though, is solely the school board's.

Governance teams may occasionally face rooms crowded with angry teachers or sobbing parents. Members of the local press often attend meetings about sensitive issues. The governance team has a great deal to do with the perceived outcome of a meeting, and those perceptions are often predicated upon the board's thoughtful responses to those angry or upset people who address the meeting. When the superintendent's recommendations are clear, the board can weigh the voices of the constituents against the recommendation of the superintendent and formulate its own conclusions.

When an agenda item is considered to be of high consequence to the organization, a superintendent may feel the need to lobby, recruit people to the cause, or advocate taking a certain position. Superintendents are hired for their passion and enthusiasm, and therefore it can be a very difficult trial when it is necessary for them to act unemotional. Nonetheless, it is the job of the superintendent to make an informed but dispassionate recommendation to the board, as well as to accept the consequences of the board's decision.

> "They know when I make a recommendation I've done my homework. When I ask for the board's support, I ask them to have a titanium backbone."—Anonymous superintendent

Every school board is as different as the members of which it is composed. It is the job of the superintendent to keep board members informed of important occurrences and events in the district in order to avoid surprises and to build a strong working relationship with each member. Some board members will want to communicate with the superintendent regularly and often. Others are far less interested in constant communication, and they may become overwhelmed by "information overload." It is an unwritten requirement of the position that superintendents need to know the communication preferences of each board member and work to accommodate members' individual styles.

Superintendents should know their boards well enough to know what information will be of interest or of concern to a particular board member. They should know about what issues individual board members are passionate, and which projects they would like to see accomplished. A knowledgeable superintendent knows the school board so well he or she can correctly anticipate how each member will vote on an issue before the item is presented.

"Gathering data about individual board members' interests, their goals, and motivations for their work on behalf of the district's children and families is essential. Without frequent personal, focused, and relaxed conversations on these topics, the superintendent cannot fully understand each board member's motivation."—Townsend et al. (2007, p. 5)

The superintendent often sets the agenda for upcoming meetings in conjunction with the board president. Naturally, this involves greater contact between the superintendent and the president than with any of the other board members.

Despite whatever differences there may be among board members' communication preferences, each member must receive the same information from the superintendent. If one member has the sense that another board member—even the president—may be receiving better information or preferential treatment from the superintendent or staff, this may cause conflicts in relationships. In order to avoid this discord, the superintendent must strive to ensure that all board members receive the same information.

One particularly effective communication solution is for the district leader to write a meeting summary and distribute it to all members following a one-on-one meeting with the board president. "Always give the board more than what they wanted," reminds Dr. Jean Fuller.

The governance team must always be fully informed, and it is a superintendent's responsibility to ensure that all board members receive the same information. Effective superintendents lay the foundation for instructional success by communicating frequently and well. Manny Barbara advises, "Let them know everything that goes on. I never hide anything from the board."

Henry Escobar, a fifteen-year superintendent, suggests, "Earn support by being competent, transparent, open, and honest."

Discussion Scenario #7:
"Above the Fold" Leadership

Early Saturday morning, Superintendent Fred Timms turned up the sidewalk as he returned from his constitutional. He sighed to himself when he noticed that the paperboy had thrown the newspaper in his wife's prized rosebushes yet again. As he reached down to pluck the paper carefully out from between the branches, the morning's headline screamed, "Trustee Dines at Kids' Expense but Won't Approve Preschool." Next to the headline was a picture of Mr. Nelson at the last board meeting. Another board member with an accusatory look on her face was pointing her finger at him. Timms yanked the paper out from the spiked branches, scattering three of the new buds onto the ground.

"Oh boy, we're above the fold," thought Superintendent Timms. "This is not good."

The room was filled to capacity at the next board meeting. The trustees, who had never before limited public comment, knew they could not begin to impose restrictions now. Parent after parent approached the microphone, often holding a child by the hand. Every parent had more or less the same comments: "My child needs preschool, and instead you're out wining and dining at our kids' expense. Shame on you!"

Timms's board had never been particularly interested in receiving board member training. Now they wished they had, because not a single member knew how best to respond. They never received coaching about how to face such anger. Instead, all they could think to do was stare down at their board packets and try their best to become invisible.

It didn't take long before the board's demeanor created even greater ire among the audience.

"You obviously don't care," screeched one mother. "You won't even look at us." Emotions ran so high that parents left the meeting plotting the recall of "Carnivore Jack."

"All I did was eat a measly steak, and now everyone's upset," Jack Nelson whined to himself. He was shocked at the vociferousness of

(continued)

the public's rage. "I work hard for these parents. They have no idea how much time and effort I put into my board work!"

The next morning when he arrived at the district office, Timms was surprised to find several parents holding picket signs. Written on them were slogans such as "Preschool for Our Kids" and "Save My Kid's Education from Being Eaten." The following day, more groups of parents similarly picketed each school in the district.

"What a thorny situation," thought Superintendent Timms. "It appears I have my work cut out for me."

Discussion Questions

- What could Superintendent Timms have done to avoid this situation?
- What discussions should the superintendent have with the board as a whole, and specifically with the targeted board member?
- What should Superintendent Timms do to quell the anger of the constituents?

Communicating well means that a prudent instructional leader will sometimes intentionally repeat important information. The school board is inundated with paperwork. It is helpful for the superintendent to reiterate key items to help the board focus. A superintendent's job is to provide the best information possible. Accurate and timely reminders about important data, facts, and issues will help the board arrive at the best possible decision.

A majority of top district leaders use a weekly letter to communicate with their boards. A weekly newsletter can be used to give the board a preview of items that will be presented at the next board meeting. Dr. Sharon Robison remarks, "An effective weekly letter gets 98 percent of the board questions out of the way."

"I operate on the premise I don't like surprises. The board doesn't either." —Dr. Nancy Carroll, thirteen-year superintendent

In some districts, no item is permitted to appear on the meeting agenda before it has been introduced to the board via the weekly newsletter. The purpose of this requirement is to ensure that board members are given plenty of opportunity to ask questions and receive additional details or explanation prior to the appearance of the item on the agenda. A preview, however, cannot take the place of a board discussion or vote, so both the sender and the recipients must be cautious to continue to follow laws and regulations for open meeting guidelines regarding agenda item discussions. Superintendents must always keep in mind that these weekly circulars may be subject to public scrutiny.

Public information requests allow the public access to most written correspondence sent to the board. It is always best to regard all written correspondence with the same level of caution. The legal definition of "written correspondence" encompasses messages sent by either electronic (e-mail) or postal mail. Never put anything in an e-mail or written newsletter that you would not want revealed on the front page of the local paper.

Superintendents must remain cognizant of the fact that documents given to board members are generally subject to public review and must therefore always be written with circumspection. Some district leaders send their weekly letters to the board by U.S. mail rather than electronically in order to avoid one of the risks associated with e-mail: it can be forwarded easily, and the originator can, with some effort, cover his or her tracks.

The school board has but a single raison d'être: student achievement. Should board members' attention waver, a superintendent must refocus their efforts on this most important work. Helping students is the reason most board members run. Supporting academic success is critical to the mission of the board. It is incumbent upon

"Most of us have been told at one time or another not to 'sweat the small stuff.' Good preparation for board meetings includes what might be viewed as 'small stuff.' But in this case it's probably a good idea to sweat it—just a bit."—Townsend et al. (2005, p. 51)

the superintendent to keep board members from becoming so distracted with the district's day-to-day operations that they might temporarily miss the bigger picture. If the district leader fails to create an infrastructure that puts issues of student success on every agenda, it becomes easy for the board to lose focus and get lost in the business and the politics of running the district.

There are many ways for an outstanding instructional leader to build energy for student and educational improvement with the school board. For instance, some outstanding superintendents begin board meetings with student performances, school reports, model lessons, or other student-focused activities. Dr. Howard Sundberg, a superintendent with over thirty years in the field of education, explains one of the reasons for his success. "We have curriculum highlights at the start of every meeting. Putting the instructional part of the meeting first shows the focus. It is also helpful in keeping the meeting positive when you start on a high note."

Even a seemingly mundane item such as the decor of the boardroom might serve as a subtle reminder to the board of where their focus ought to lie. Top instructional superintendents often ensure boardrooms are staged to showcase student work and highlight recent educational accomplishments.

Top superintendents often ask school representatives to post student work or present their current efforts, assessment results, or benchmarks during a board meeting. The presence of student work and the reporting of student academic progress during each board meeting serve as constant reminders of the primacy of the district's goal of increasing achievement. A powerful and effective instructional leader understands that one key to building a strong framework for student achievement is to make that achievement the foundation of every board agenda.

BUILDING SOLUTIONS TO BOARD DYSFUNCTION

Board members who want to micromanage and solve problems that should be solved by staff are a common problem for superintendents. Board members may genuinely believe they are being inquisitive and helpful when in fact they are overstepping their bounds. It is often a thorny issue to help board members understand this fact, and unfortunately it is usually even more difficult to persuade them to stop. There is

"Pick your board very carefully. Find out what their motives are before you work for them."—Dr. Jack Gyves

at least one effective way to handle situations of board micromanagement. Suggests one superintendent, "I tell board members, 'You don't want this problem. Kick it back to me and I will handle it.'"

Another example of boardsmanship gone awry is when an individual board member begins demanding things without the agreement of the rest of the board. A board meeting may be running smoothly when an individual board member asks for a report, requests a purchase, or directs the superintendent to perform a task. This lone board member understandably leaves the superintendent wondering what to do next. In the words of one superintendent, "In a meeting when a board member says, 'I'd like this,' I say nothing and wait for someone else to support it. I ask for the consensus of the board. That way, I avoid working for five boards."

Should a superintendent find that the board repeatedly ignores his recommendations, it may be time to seek out a position in a new district. At times, many superintendents find certain issues trigger profound emotional responses because of their personal core beliefs, and often they feel compelled to stand up for their viewpoint even when their cause is demonstrably lost. To think around this issue, one experienced superintendent reminds leaders to ask themselves, "What bridge am I willing to die on? If this is it, understand that you may not be superintendent after that, but you will be lauded as someone who did the right thing."

Applicants for a superintendent position have a personal responsibility to ensure the best match between themselves and the school district. The best way to do this is simply by researching the position and the district, and by responding truthfully in the interview. Being honest throughout the hiring process is not only common sense; it is also the only ethically responsible way to obtain one's next position.

Without the ethical component, one's sense of legitimacy and accomplishment can be severely compromised to the detriment of both the district and the superintendent's career.

"When applying for the job, it is critical you answer what you really believe, not what you think they want to hear," says one superintendent, "because your alignment with the board is critical. They need to know who you are. If they hire you, they saw alignment. If they did not hire you, it means you were not a match."

A lack of research leaves one at a disadvantage when one is attempting to make a decision. Superintendent candidates must attempt to learn as much as possible about the sitting school board in any district in which they seek a position. One long-term superintendent says, "One-third of all school boards you would kill to work with. One-third have one or two mavericks, and one-third are totally dysfunctional."

The interview and hiring process is a two-way street. The candidate chooses the board, inasmuch as the board chooses the superintendent. One would do well to remember that likely there are multiple applicants for the position. It is each candidate's responsibility to query the board and to ask relevant questions. Absent this, it is unlikely an aspirant can best choose a board with which to work.

> "I have often heard administrators say that when it's not fun anymore they will leave. Being a superintendent is rarely fun. It is a challenging, satisfying, rewarding, confounding, and incomparable experience, but rarely fun."— Johnson et al. (2002, p. 122)

The school board can make or break the success of a superintendent. If a school board ceases to function effectively, so does the district. If a candidate encounters a dysfunctional board during the interview process, he or she would be wise to reconsider the desirability of the position. If during one's superintendency a board becomes dysfunctional, one should conduct a critical analysis of the feasibility of continuing in that position. The board must approve almost everything the district leader attempts to accomplish. Sadly, this makes some board problems insurmountable.

Problems on the board should be neither ignored nor avoided. Issues must be addressed and resolved as soon as practicable. Infighting among members impacts the board and the governance team, and it can negatively impact the district by ceasing its march

"True leadership shows up in adverse times."—Dr. Darline Robles

toward progress. "When a board is going sideways, it is because the adults are fussing at each other," observes one superintendent.

It is an unfortunate fact that the superintendent, who works for the board, also must help rectify its shortcomings. A superintendent might solicit the assistance of the board president in confronting poor behavior on the part of a board member. Other times, the president is a part of the problem. In either case, poor behavior cannot be permitted to continue. The superintendent should take steps to address bad behavior firmly, but also in the most people-friendly method possible. One effective solution may be to hold one-on-one meetings with a board member. Depending on the scope of the issue, it may even require the help of an outside consultant.

There is a saying, "Conflict is like a mushroom; it grows in the dark." Board unrest casts shadows throughout the district and brings the district's most important work to a halt. When there is a conflict on the board, it is best for the superintendent to help bring the issues to light and to resolve them rather than allowing them to continue or to hope they solve themselves.

Dysfunctional boards can assume many forms and evince a variety of symptoms. Direct hostility (of members toward one another, of the board toward the superintendent, or toward a third party), passive-aggressive behavior, or the intentional monopolization of staff time with no clear objective in mind are some of the more common manifestations of board malfunction. One of the more profound ramifications of a dysfunctional board is that the superintendent and staff are rendered unable to conduct important business, and district progress crawls to a stop.

If you should find yourself promoted to superintendent upon a superior's termination, one veteran leader urges, "Get your board under control, fast!" Once an internecine battle has begun, war within the school board can continue indefinitely. A wise superintendent will sidestep this battle by redirecting the focus of the board to where it must be: on the students. "I've spent a lot of time brokering relationships between adults, and I don't want to do that anymore," says one superintendent.

There is far too much important work to accomplish for a school board to spend its time on power struggles. Sometimes the goals the district fails to meet can negatively impact multiple parties within the district: the superintendent, staff, faculty, and students. A string of conspicuous failures will embarrass the board as well. "I try to make it clear to the board that enlightened self-interest would get them behind instruction, otherwise the district would be under sanctions," says one superintendent.

> "One superintendent of a very high-achieving district told us he had two rules: 1. Everything is an issue; 2. When you think something is not going to be an issue, see rule number one."—Townsend et al. (2005, p. 65)

Recurring disagreements between a superintendent and a majority of the school board may mean that there is nothing a leader can do to facilitate a change dramatic enough to make the team function effectively. The standard by which a degree of dysfunction can be measured is to ask, "Are we able to reach the goals we need to reach in order to do what is best for our students?" If the answer is "no," the only recourse the superintendent may have is to start looking for another position.

Most superintendents will encounter a maverick board member from time to time. Often this individual takes the guise of a bully. This person has a personal agenda and plans to carry it out, regardless of the consequences. No matter the issue, when the rest of the board leans one way, the maverick will lean another.

Top superintendents suggest that one can attempt to remedy the situation by making a genuine effort to connect with the oppositional board member on a personal level. If this tactic fails, a superintendent may have no other option but to consult with the board president. If the maverick is the board president, then one

---

Discussion Scenario #8:
A Challenge of Purple Proportions

Almost as soon as she finished reading the want ads, Dr. Anita Cava-naugh began her research about the open superintendent position. She drove around the area, subscribed to the local paper, and even spoke with the departing superintendent. "It's a great little district," the former superintendent told her. "But the board is a challenge."

"How hard can it be?" thought Anita. "I would only have to meet with the board every two weeks, and between those meetings I'd be free to work on my effective instructional leadership skills. Besides, I hear the students and staff are pleasant and friendly, and the schools are doing well. I want this job!"

Anita was hired as superintendent, and her new staff pledged their support. Most mentioned to the new superintendent they thought she would like the school and the community. But Anita soon picked up a subtle message. Not one person ever mentioned she would like working with the school board. This absence of comment insinuated to Anita that she had perhaps inherited a difficult board along with her new job.

Toward the end of her first board meeting, Rich Parker, the board president, raised an idea that was not on the agenda. "I think we should paint the high school bright purple, to match the school colors."

"What are you, Rich, nuts?" asked one board member.

"We have our image to keep up!" added another.

On it went for over ninety minutes. The meeting was finally adjourned with no conclusion to Mr. Parker's proposal.

The new superintendent contemplated the evening's events on her drive home. "Two hours! For an item that wasn't even on the agenda! Wow, we have a lot of training to do."

The next morning, the board president showed up at the high school in his truck carrying a fifteen-foot ladder and a bucket of bright purple paint. When Anita confronted Mr. Parker and asked what he was doing, he replied, "I've come to paint the walls purple, like we agreed last night."

(continued)

"But we didn't come to agreement, or even take a vote," said Anita.

"Too bad. What are you going to do to stop me, Dr. Cavanaugh?" sneered the president.

"That's a good question," the beleaguered superintendent mused.

Discussion Questions

- What issues does Dr. Cavanaugh face in regard to working with her board?
- What is the heart of the problem?
- What should she do next?

should discuss the situation with one's fellow superintendents and solicit their advice regarding how to best proceed.

Superintendents who have experienced a maverick or bully firsthand also caution not to take conflicts personally. In the words of one superintendent, "You cannot take responsibility for a board member's behavior. If they take in the information and nothing connects, it is not your fault. When you have someone undermining you, you have to take the high ground."

> "I had one bully on the board. She drew the line in the sand and said, 'You guys just need to get on the same plan.' I said to her, 'I'll do my best to balance the issues. I must hear all five voices.' I couldn't believe adults would behave that way."—Anonymous superintendent

A good board will confront the issue of a bullying member and correct the problem in closed session. Dr. Sharon Robison reminds superintendents, "You don't work for one member of the board. You work for the board. If one person is throwing bullets or darts, you have to speak with the president. You can't reprimand your boss. You must go to your board and then back off."

The community selects a school board, and the board reflects the views of the voters. In some cases, the board will come to conclusions or decide upon policies that the superintendent cannot in good conscience support. If events come to this, the superintendent may have no choice other than to leave. "If you can't do what the board is asking you to do, you need to get out," advises one superintendent.

One may not always be able to fix a dysfunctional school board. Said one respondent, "If you find yourself in a wagon with four wheels with some going one way and some going the other way, you're going nowhere. Get out."

A split board can cripple a superintendent, and over time the position can become untenable. "People get power bases built up, and they are not about to let go," explained one past superintendent. Another leader recalled ruefully, "I realized working with my board was like trying to drive with a flat tire."

> "If you think there is a war between factions, I would get my résumé together and leave on my own terms. Because a head will roll if there is a war, and if you are the superintendent, it will be yours."—Anonymous superintendent

It is one thing to work with a school board that recognizes it has problems and struggles to overcome them. Some boards, though, do not want to fix their own problems. A few may deny there are any significant issues at all, and still others seem to prefer creating crises rather than solving them.

When one encounters opposition meeting after meeting, or if there seems to be an ongoing and unresolved fight between board factions rather than a focus on student achievement, it may be time to pull the plug and begin polishing one's résumé. The only other option, in the words of one top leader, is "You can hedge your bets and ask yourself if you can outwait them."

It is difficult to know if—or when—an adverse situation will resolve itself, or if it will instead continue indefinitely. One former award-winning superintendent explains, "During my career I've had two boards on which I had someone undermining me every day. But I kept doing my work. I told myself if I have to continually battle, I'm going to do something else for a living."

CONCLUSION

The partnership of the school board and the superintendent is of critical importance to the successful operation of the school district. When the delicate balance of authority falls out of alignment, the governance team structure will inexorably weaken and, if not corrected, eventually fail. Without a strong underpinning on which to build, the students will eventually bear the weight of the governance team's failure.

Strong communication, board education and training, and carefully crafting solutions to board dysfunction are important in the quest for instructional leadership. Attention to the articulated and intrinsic needs of the governance team will increase a superintendent's chances of success, by creating a well-trained and high-functioning board composed of persons who understand their role as school board members.

Not all problems with a school board can be solved. In the words of a wise top superintendent: "In cases like this, you need to be able to count to three." That is, if you cannot rely on the consistent support of at least three board members, there is no choice. It is time to go.

IMPLICATIONS FOR ACTION

- Together, the superintendent and the board constitute the governance team.
- The superintendent works for the board, not the other way around. Superintendents do not ultimately set the direction of the district.
- It is the superintendent's role to hire staff.
- Develop a "floating bottom line" in order to remain flexible and in alignment with the board.
- Effective board members begin as learners and become leaders. Arrange for regular governance training for the school board.

Be sure to train candidates, as well as new board members. Have ongoing refresher training for sitting board members.

- Effective instructional leaders know, understand, and gear their communication style to the preferences of each board member.
- Ensure that all members of the board are fully and equally informed.
- Guide the board by reiterating key points and highlighting important issues.
- When the superintendent and board do not agree on an issue even after the superintendent has made clear her views and recommendations, then the superintendent needs to accept the decision of the board.
- Address problems and difficult behaviors among the members of the board.
- Prospective superintendents must choose their district wisely. As much as possible, ask questions of the board throughout the interview process.
- Remember that not all problems can be solved. In some instances, a superintendent's only rational response to board conflict is to seek a new position.

4

PERSONNEL ISSUES

The importance of hiring the right personnel should not be underestimated. Effective educational leaders build their teams by hiring effective employees, and they have the courage to terminate substandard staff members. While hiring and firing generally falls under the auspices of the personnel office, top employee recruitment, development, and retention are of critical importance to the success of the superintendent.

Leaders create change for students by ensuring that there are high-quality teachers in every classroom. The pace of this effort, however, is worthy of consideration. "Remember, you are dealing equally with people and progress," advises Dr. Louise Taylor. "We've seen people who focus only on progress, and they roll over people with it. We have seen those people who focus only on people, and they get no progress. Effective leaders need both."

How do effective leaders determine the "right" pace of change? To best gauge progress, one ought to seek the opinions of those who are most trusted in the administration. Speaking with the staff in confidence, and in a low-key manner, is generally the best way to take the temperature of the organization without creating undue angst. Use these meetings as an opportunity to determine how the pace of change is affecting staff members personally and professionally, how the organizational transformation feels, and what they have heard others saying. Reassure them that their opinions are valuable, and reiterate that the conversation is strictly "off the record."

It is of the utmost importance to recognize that hiring, firing, and replacing personnel is more than filling slots or adding new faces. Effective leaders must understand the effects caused by personnel changes, and that there may be a need to modify the rate of change to mitigate the magnitude of that impact. Superintendents are sometimes described as "change enthusiasts." However, most people prefer the status quo to living with, or through, change. Monitor the pace of change, and moderate it, within limits, according to the needs of the organization.

> "We expected that good-to-great leaders would begin by setting a new vision and strategy. We found instead that they first got the right people on the bus, the wrong people off the bus, and the right people in the right seats on the bus—and then they figured out where to drive it. The old adage 'People are your most important asset' turns out to be wrong. People are not your most important asset. The right people are."—Collins (2001, p. 13)

Finding and recruiting the best candidates is a rather arduous task. Great people do not usually just walk in the door. True, some districts seem to have very little trouble finding well-qualified personnel. In others, recruiting is a constant source of difficulty.

Some superintendents tenaciously recruit staff members from nearby districts. "We aggressively recruit in other districts. We make calls directly and ask people to apply," confided one top leader. While this approach can be effective in finding new or better staff, one must also exercise a great deal of caution in using this style of unabashed recruiting. One's district may be able to attract better teachers, but this approach will likely not lend itself to warm and friendly relations with neighboring superintendents.

Superintendents might find it helpful to spread positive words about their district in order to enhance its public image and facilitate recruiting. Creating an environment that is perceived to be a great place in which to work will facilitate finding and hiring the best candidates. "We've put together a recruiting packet," says John Aycock. "It contains our points of pride. We put this out with all the realtors in town. A big part of the recruiting effort is image building. We have a reputation of being a great place to work."

Newsletters, booths at local events, and public speeches by the superintendent are all wonderful ways to enhance the image of your district. At the same time, leaders should be careful not to "oversell" or otherwise unintentionally mislead prospective candidates. Promising more than the district can deliver can lead to suboptimal outcomes for the new candidate, the organization, and the superintendent.

> "The people closest to him determine every leader's potential. If those people are strong, then the leader can make a huge impact. If they are weak, he can't."—Maxwell (1998, p. 110)

It is the job of the superintendent to be sure candidates have a realistic expectation of what they will find when they arrive. If recruitment materials paint an unrealistic or partial picture, a new hire's experiences in the district will quite likely be off to a poor start.

For example, many teachers in one remote school district moved there from the Midwest. They were enticed by a promise that the region was "an hour from the beach, the mountains, and cultural activities." Imagine each new employee's surprise as he pulled into that rural desert community for the first time. The district was in fact an hour from the beach, the mountains, and from cultural activities, and there was no outright deception involved in the recruitment materials. But what the prospective candidates were not told was that the district was in the middle of the desert, and the scenery included Joshua trees, tumbleweeds, and the occasional coyote.

There are many opinions about the "best" qualities and characteristics that district leaders should look for in teaching candidates. Interestingly, top superintendents do not make teaching proficiency the primary characteristic they seek when hiring new faculty members. "The first filter should be to hire people who are honest, trustworthy, and fair," says Dr. Jean Fuller. "I used to hire for competence, but I found that honesty, trustworthiness, and fairness were more important."

Effective instructional leaders should aim to recruit teachers who will make the best match for the organization. "We make sure people know who we are," says Becci Gillespie, who has seven years of experience as a superintendent. "When we are hiring, we explain that we have a strong core. To put it directly, we're not changing for you."

Being clear about the expectations and culture of a district allows a superintendent to discern those candidates who will likely best fit the district from those who may not. It is no surprise that the hiring process is most effective when it is conducted in a thoughtful and unhurried manner. No methodology is foolproof, but taking the time to use a variety of recruitment techniques or approaches increases the chances the process will yield a better candidate match.

Regina Rossall, a superintendent with more than thirty years of experience in the field of education, attempts to ensure a good match in her district by putting candidates through a rigorous interview process. Her methods work in her district because she puts a premium on expertise in addition to best fit. "Before we hire teachers, they work with us for a day as part of the interview. We want to see what they do in this environment. We have teachers do a model lesson for us."

Recruiting outstanding faculty is only the first half of the battle to create a high-functioning school district. A good leader must not only be able to hire top candidates, but must also ensure as much as possible that the new employees will want to remain with the organization. Henry Escobar advocates a straightforward solution: give teachers the resources and tools they need to do their jobs. He says, "My first year as a teacher, I had to buy resources for the classroom out of my own pocket. There is no reason for a teacher to spend

"Between recruiting and retention, retention is more important. We have created a whole menu of things to get them to stay. We must be competitive."—Ned McNabb, experienced rural district superintendent

a dime of his or her own pay. We believe people need to have the tools to do the job."

There is a combination of extrinsic and intrinsic rewards that makes people comfortable staying with a particular employer. There is much more to retaining good teachers than pay. Superintendent Ned McNabb understands this firsthand. "Fundamentally, good teachers must be at a place where they can teach effectively. Never underestimate the power of a teacher liking where they teach. If you give them good principals, nice rooms, a good campus, safety and supplies, it goes a long way to making teachers feel valued and supported."

McNabb puts his philosophy into practice by seeking to connect with teachers in his district on an individual basis. His efforts are predicated on the thought that making an ongoing investment in building a personal relationship can yield big dividends in retaining staff. "When I talk with teachers, I tell them how much I appreciate them," he says.

EMPLOYEE EVALUATION

The importance of making timely, fact-based, and clear employee evaluations cannot be overemphasized. But how ought a leader define employee success? What characteristics, actions, or habits make an employee effective? How is success defined and measured? Perhaps more important, by what measure does an exceptional instructional leader determine the difference between an effective employee and one who is not?

> "There is something within us that responds deeply to people who level with us."—Scott (2002, p. 18)

A seasoned administrator does not have to spend a long time in the classroom of a struggling teacher to know there is a problem. Experts agree that good teachers bring a blend of aptitude, attitude, and personality to the position. "You can't teach people qualities like attitude, enthusiasm, and caring. You cannot develop these things in people. They must have them inherently. You can teach people how to teach reading, but you can't teach them to have a good attitude," says Richard Bray, liaison to the California Board of Education and the No Child Left Behind Task Force.

It is axiomatic that every experienced administrator has encountered people in the profession who truly do not seem to enjoy working with children. "If you don't like kids, that's a problem," warns one leader. "Even if you don't like kids, I ask people to try to act like they do."

Good teachers also require a certain amount of inherent talent. Dr. Dennis Fox says, "We must distinguish between knowledge and skills versus aptitude. Knowledge and skills can be taught. Hard wiring can only be changed so much. The leader must determine, 'Is the problem that they don't know what to do, or is it just because of who they are?'"

It is common for superintendents to hold individual meetings regularly with principals, or to charge high-ranking members of their cabinet with the responsibility to do so. One district superintendent schedules time with principals every month. At each meeting, this instructional leader reviews the performance of faculty members. Because of the information he learns during on-site visits, that superintendent is familiar with the teaching staff, and visiting classrooms gives him a basis from which he and the principal can engage in a meaningful dialogue about each employee's effectiveness.

Instructional superintendents develop and implement systems of internal accountability for teacher evaluation. Incompetent faculty members should not be allowed to work in one's school district. If an employee becomes a subject of concern, it is the superintendent's responsibility to ensure that the principal documents evidence of that employee's nonperformance. Keeping written records is integral to building a successful case for employee non-reelection. Written documentation is also important to protect the school, the principal, the superintendent, the district, and ultimately, the school board from legal ramifications.

Once it has been determined there is a significant problem with a teacher, management intervention is critical. Often, superintendents are required by review boards to show they have attempted to work with the individual and remediate the problem. "If they are not meeting our standards, we put them in PAR [Peer Assistance and Review Program]. If things do not change, we go for dismissal," says one superintendent. Whether a faculty member's shortcoming is due to poor aptitude or bad attitude, "Our bottom line question is, 'Would you put your child in this person's classroom?' If not, there is something radically wrong with you keeping them."

"We put a lot of pressure on by spending a lot of time in classrooms where the teacher is not making it," says another superintendent. "If they are not making it, we get rid of them in year one. Principals are held under the gun by me. I do their yearly evaluation. I don't show any mercy if the principal should have let someone go and they didn't."

COPING WITH SUBSTANDARD EMPLOYEES

Site leadership is the key to academic achievement within the school building, and school principals are a critical link to student success. Effective instructional superintendents should strive to set up a written employee management system and include within it provisions for evaluating and documenting substandard employees.

Key components of an effective review program that emphasizes internal accountability include a reporting mechanism that requires administrators to submit evaluations or other written records to the superintendent or superintendent's designee, as well as specific time frames in which changes are required. Absent an information and management system incorporating written documentation and timelines, it is highly unlikely that personnel files will adequately reflect the performance of poor employees. Inadequate or improper record keeping makes terminating substandard workers extremely difficult.

Firing employees is difficult and often painful, but is one of the most important responsibilities of an instructional leader. Retaining poor employees, and bad teachers in particular, negatively impacts students by Malthusian proportions. A single principal who fails to eliminate poorly performing teachers will not only profoundly impact the educational experience of the students at that school, but over time this neglect will also have a negative effect on the district's overall performance. Such irresponsibility leaves an entire district vulnerable to increased scrutiny and even to possible sanction. One should adopt the motto, "When in doubt, send them out."

Instructional leaders proactively coach and monitor their principals in order to ensure that new teachers who prove themselves unsuitable are not reelected. One must remember that effective superintendents manage the termination schedule and process. They are not carried along by it. "I don't take pride in getting rid of people, but I also don't hesitate to let people go," explained one superintendent.

If a principal is indecisive or seems reluctant to dismiss a poor teacher, the superintendent is obligated to remind that principal, emphatically and often, that it is their duty to let the faculty member go. "Document [the teacher]," says one leader. "If the person is really poor, you can get rid of that person. You must have the courage to do that."

A superior instructional superintendent will not leave the faculty evaluation process solely to a site administrator. "During the site visits, if I see a teacher who is not satisfactory, I go to the principal's office," says one superintendent. "I'll ask what's going on. It is rare that I walk into an unsatisfactory classroom and find that the principal doesn't know about the problem. The principals develop a remediation plan. We discuss the evaluation."

Firing people is one of the most difficult functions of a leader, but it is one of the most critical. In the words of one administrator, "Sometimes you inherit people you wouldn't have picked. Sometimes you have to 'unpick' them. Let people go with dignity. When we let people go, I say, 'Look, I don't want to fire you. You can resign and ask for another assignment, and when you're asked, say, "Yes,

I chose this assignment.'" People leave a letter with me. I give them the option to walk out the door on their own two feet. You can't destroy someone's reputation. It doesn't help you at all."

Terminating less-than-effective employees is often messy. Faculty and staff loyalties can be torn, and emotions can run hot. Few experienced administrators have not borne witness to the phenomenon of displays of irrational loyalty to a departing staff member. A teacher who might ordinarily despise another faculty member can become that person's loudest advocate during a termination effort.

> "Realize that no support system will compensate for bad teaching."
> —DuFour et al. (2006, p. 85)

The more networked an employee is within the organization, the more likely it is that board meetings will be filled with rancor and heated discussion if that person is let go. As illogical as it may be, this mind-set is analogous to the sentiment "I can say bad things about my spouse/sibling/friend. But don't YOU dare say anything bad about them!"

Superintendents and principals will rarely wonder what others may think about a termination decision. "Supporters show up to complain when you take action, regardless of how much other people indicated they wanted the person gone," sighs one superintendent. It is almost as predictable, though, that some teachers will pull a principal aside to thank him for moving a poor teacher along.

Astute teachers know who among their co-workers is not performing. They are likely frustrated by the negative impact this underperforming faculty member has on the students and on the academic reputation of the school. Most people are loath to express negative thoughts aloud. Principals and instructional superintendents can rest assured that the school faculty, however silent, appreciates the effort at institutional improvement.

Often an honest conversation about their poor performance may be enough to encourage a new or deficient teacher to consider another career. One superintendent who prefers to remain anonymous describes her technique: "I make bad teachers intentionally

Discussion Scenario #9: The Mess

When she opened the door to Ms. Lopez's classroom, district super-intendent Dr. Shayna Brown immediately saw the teacher had no control of the learning process.

The superintendent ducked as a paper airplane sailed by her head. Ms. Lopez apparently saw the plane too but chose to ignore it. It seemed as though the teacher was making a sincere effort to engage the few children who were paying attention. Unfortunately, it was also apparent that no matter how hard the teacher tried, no learning was going on.

After spending less than ten minutes in the class, Dr. Brown had seen more than enough. She left the classroom and strode purpose-fully down the hallway and into Principal Matt Sloan's office. After exchanging a few pleasantries, the superintendent addressed the subject at hand.

"What is being done about Carlotta Lopez?" she asked.

"Ms. Lopez is in the Beginning Teacher Training Program. Our instructional coach works with her, and I am in her classroom almost every day. We've all coached her on what needs to be done, but she just doesn't seem to have the ability to do the job," explained Princi-pal Sloan. "Here's the improvement plan we have for her."

Dr. Brown scanned the paper. "Hmmm . . . tardiness . . . lack of control . . . ineffective . . ." She looked up and asked the principal, "You're prepared to let her go at year end?"

"More than prepared," he responded. "To keep a lid on things in the meantime we've assigned a long-term substitute to assist in that classroom. It will be expensive, but what else can we do? The kids are missing out."

"You know that there will be a lot of teachers who may not think she's any good, but they won't want to see her let go, either, right, Matt?" inquired the superintendent.

The principal shook his head ruefully. "That's always the way. There has to be a way to terminate an ineffective staff member with-out upsetting everyone else here. Any suggestions, Dr. Brown?"

Discussion Questions

- How might Superintendent Brown help Principal Sloan prepare for Ms. Lopez's termination?
- Define the possible negative and positive short-term ramifications of terminating a teacher such as Ms. Lopez: on students, faculty, and the community. What are the long-term effects?
- Thinking about the response to the previous question, do some consequences outweigh the others? Which are most important? Why?

uncomfortable. I do less and less shielding of people. I try to buy them out. I say, 'I know you're not happy here. This is the evidence I see. Is there something you would rather do? How can we both win here?'"

It takes courage to eliminate substandard employees from the workplace. Effective instructional leaders must embrace the challenge to remove poor employees from the district. Once inadequate teachers are purged, ones who are more effective in working with students can replace them.

HIRING INSTRUCTIONAL LEADERS

The superintendent plays an integral part in the process of selecting principals and assistant principals. Effective instructional leaders must understand that, in addition to hiring and retaining outstanding faculty, it is no less important to hire exceptional administrators.

District leaders must keep uppermost in mind the thought that hiring the "best of the best" is critical to successfully fulfilling their mission of improving student achievement. To achieve that goal, superintendents would be well advised to look for principals and assistants who

> "Always stay close to the process of hiring and evaluating principals. Never let that get away from you."—Jim Brown

exhibit personal and professional characteristics such as energy, optimism, determination, and passion. One rule of thumb is that if a potential candidate seems merely adequate, that person ought not to be hired. It is impossible to create excellent schools with only passable principals.

Most superintendents select school administrators by setting up interview panels made up of members of the teachers' union, the classified union, parents, teachers, community members, and even people from the prospective administrator's site. Using a broad base of blocs will ensure adequate consideration of a variety of perspectives.

Ensuring opportunity of input from diverse groups can be achieved in any number of ways. One district chooses to operate two simultaneous interview panels, each composed of people representing different factions or perspectives. The rationale for using two panels is that it allows each candidate multiple attempts to make a good impression. This approach also encourages as much input as practicable from multiple constituents early in the process.

Candidates meet with each panel in succession. Each group asks separate questions. Afterward, the scores from both are tallied, and the superintendent and executive cabinet subsequently interview those candidates who score in the top three.

Consensus arising from a collection of viewpoints makes board buy-in more likely. Ensuring early input from a diverse assortment of individuals can be very useful to quell controversies later in the process. When union leadership is involved early in the process, for example, it will be problematic for employees to later contend that they were not represented in employment decisions.

Irrespective of the number of interview panels or the constituencies involved, the strengths of each prospective candidate and how those qualities will mesh with those of the rest of the team ought to be the ultimate arbiter when making the final selection. "Hire people that will add to your strengths," counsels one superintendent. "I know what my weaknesses are. I want someone who will complement me. I look for people who can see the big picture."

DEALING WITH SUBSTANDARD ADMINISTRATORS

The function of an administrator is to effectively lead others as well as to adequately manage himself. Occasionally a superintendent may come to the uneasy realization that there are many complaints emanating from a single site, and that those complaints concern a specific person. In circumstances like this, often that person is the school's principal. To remedy the situation, "I give them very specific things they have to fix," says one superintendent. "We have to remember at the end of the day, who suffers. Kids and teachers. That makes the uncomfortable conversations easier to have."

> "The moment you feel the need to tightly manage someone, you've made a hiring mistake. The best people don't need to be managed. Guided, taught, led—yes. But not tightly managed."—Collins (2001, p. 56)

Sometimes a principal's management ability will not be an issue. Occasionally the concern is one of a lack of leadership. Some principals are slow to implement change, and others may instead engage in outright opposition to any *modus operandi* other than that of business as usual. A superintendent should not hesitate to demand change if he feels that his authority is being purposefully undermined. "I had to get rid of administrators that were not on board. I had to say, 'This is the track we're going down. You're not going to stand in front of the train,'" recalled a former district leader.

The school board must support the superintendent's proposed moves regarding any impending change. One superintendent describes how he prepared the board for the termination of a site administrator: "I went in to see the school board first. I let them know that I was working with this principal. I told them my concerns. I kept them apprised of progress. Usually they are supportive because it is not a surprise. But you must have the trust of your board."

"I have replaced and moved principals," says another superintendent. "I communicate with the board early on about this. It is a running conversation. I might tell them as much as a year ahead."

Discussion Scenario #10:
Show Me the Documentation

"We are the highest poverty school in the district," Principal Peter Wheaton moaned to the superintendent. "We need to offload some of our less effective teachers in order to make space for teachers who can actually teach. Nobody plans to move this year, and we'll never improve if we can't infuse some energy around here."

"All right, Pete. Show me how you rank your teachers," responded Superintendent Sharon Brown.

The principal pulled out a sheet of paper and passed it across the desk. "Here. My best is at the top of the page, working down from there. I also gave them letter grades."

The superintendent looked intently at the sheet. "I see that you have eight 'A' teachers, ten 'C' teachers, and four 'F' teachers," observed the superintendent. "Let me see your documentation for those who are struggling."

The principal gave a bit of a shrug, and he felt his cheeks redden. "Well, Dr. Brown, if you put too much in writing, the teachers get upset and angry, and it gets pretty hard to get anything done."

Superintendent Brown arched her eyebrows in surprise. Principal Wheaton babbled on. "Besides, Sharon, nothing ever seems to come from documenting poor-performing employees. I tried for a while, but I guess at some point . . ." He trailed off weakly as the superintendent looked at him askance.

"You're asking me to move four teachers when you haven't even bothered to document your dissatisfaction with their performance?" chided Dr. Brown. "It seems to me that the problem with student achievement at this school might not rest entirely with ineffective teachers. I am starting to think that the real problem might be an ineffective principal."

Wheaton shook his head in protest as the superintendent continued, "Pete, I like you. But I don't think you left me any choice here. I will be forwarding you a document outlining my dissatisfaction with your performance. If it helps, I'll also add some examples of what I believe correctly completed documentation looks like. I don't want this to escalate, but you need to think seriously about how your lack of action has negatively impacted our students."

Discussion Questions

- What steps should Principal Wheaton have taken to properly document the struggling teachers?
- If Principal Wheaton had completed his documentation of the poorly performing teachers, would it have been appropriate for Dr. Brown to agree to move them to other sites?
- If you were Peter Wheaton, what would be your plan of action? What if you were Superintendent Brown?

The board is of critical importance in the process of eliminating poor principals. Superintendents new to a district must be vigilant and exercise caution. Occasionally there may be issues of which one is not aware. "If a superintendent arrives at a district, and the board has a hit list, don't do it. Make your own assessment," advises an experienced superintendent.

"I have learned we're in a people business," explains another district leader. "Relationships matter. In terms of letting a principal go, don't just go in and blast the place. Honor time. Time, however, is not an entitlement to continue with the same behavior."

CONCLUSION

The critical work of an instructional superintendent cannot be accomplished alone. Building a strong district is accomplished only by having a high-performing team upon which one can rely. One cannot build a district that functions well without hiring good employees and firing those who are less than effective. Strong leadership is essential to student success.

> "When you become a leader, you lose the right to think about yourself."—Gerald Brooks (quoted in Maxwell 1998, p. 189)

Retaining good people and jettisoning lower performers is paramount to the success of one's board, one's district, and one's career. Hiring, firing, and evaluating district employees are areas in which a successful and effective instructional leader must actively participate. Ongoing supervisory review is necessary to ensure strength and stability. Attracting and retaining high-quality educators and administrators is critical to accomplishing the objective of improving student achievement. A superintendent must be actively involved in the process and retain the final say in the decision.

IMPLICATIONS FOR ACTION

- Remember to deal equally with people, process, and progress.
- Be aware of the pace of change: do not roll over people, but always continue to press forward.
- Create a district for which employees want to work. One can demonstrate to employees they are valued not only through their compensation, but also in other ways, such as the look of the school grounds, ensuring there are adequate resources in the classrooms, and by using their time effectively.
- Hiring and retaining good faculty and administrative staff candidates and firing those who perform poorly is critically important. One's employees will ultimately affect one's own success.
- Hire those who will be a match with the organization and who have skills complementary to one's own.
- Evaluate both principals and teachers regularly and consistently. Let them know the results. Keep only the best.
- Have the courage to "unpick" substandard faculty and administrators.

5

INSTRUCTIONAL
LEADERSHIP

*In order to see instruction clearly, the leader must stand in
the classroom and look back up the system.*

—Dr. Juli Quinn

GOAL SHARING

Effective superintendents build a culture of continuous improvement. Says Dr. Juli Quinn, "When we can stand in the classroom
and look back up the system and see the work of everyone from the
superintendent to the custodian is aligned to improve things for
students, we will know our alignment is true."

In the words of Dr. Dennis Fox, "If instruction in the classroom
doesn't improve, nothing else matters."

What distinguishes a worthy goal from one that is less so? What
does goal setting look like when it is done right? Those answers
vary from district to district. New superintendents might develop a
laundry list of the changes they would like to implement, but they
must always be mindful that the school board sets the direction for
the district. No matter the goals one has for one's administration, it

must always be kept in mind that the board sets goals for the superintendent, not the other way around.

The school board and superintendent should spend time listening to constituents when setting objectives for the district. Community input serves as a valuable springboard from which goals can be set. Susan Custer, a former consultant in the area of school improvement for the Los Angeles County Office of Education, reminds those wishing to become instructional leaders, "Include the principals and directors in the discussion about goals for the coming years. When this is not done, the goals are not accepted by the site administrators, and the superintendent has difficulty being successful."

The board should adopt no more than six goals. Dr. Sharon Robison advises, "Board priorities should be only four to six, total. Agree and adopt. Then you can say, 'This is what I'm working on.' You can bring reports back to show you heard them and you are listening."

Working on too many goals at one time makes it difficult to focus. Dr. Ron Leon, an experienced leader who coaches and mentors superintendents, cautions that as one engages in the goal-setting process, "it is tempting—when something exciting comes along—to say, 'let's do this too.' If you take on too much, it can carry you away. You have to limit it."

"Every May I bring the leadership team in to chart what we've accomplished," says Dr. Kent Bechler. "Where is our progress? Where are our gaps? What do they think our focus should be for the next year? The management team works throughout the summer to develop goals for each department . . . then in August I hold a dinner and they report to the board, one board member at each table. It is a rotating seating arrangement, so the schools give their reports five times. This gives board members the chance to ask questions. There is a consciousness that our goals matter."

Unless there is a participative goal-setting process, a superintendent might want to head in one direction while the board follows a different roadmap. It is important that both the school board and superintendent agree with the objectives, and that everyone understands the direction in which the district will be moving. Failure to develop shared goals will inevitably lead to parties working at cross-purposes.

Discussion Scenario #11:
Role Confusion in River Rock

"I am excited to be working in River Rock School District," said district superintendent Henry Harvender in his first meeting with board president Amy Han. "I have lots of really great ideas. I've heard from many people, and I'm ready to make positive changes. This is going to be great!"

Ms. Han felt her uneasiness grow. Finally, she could contain herself no longer. "Henry, what changes do you have in mind?"

"Well, to start with, the teachers are really feeling underappreciated. We're going to need to really shore things up, so I'm planning some changes in how we negotiate. I thought I would go in and work with the teachers myself. Sometimes using an attorney can really get in the way of positive relations. I'm hoping to adjust the calendar so teachers can take their vacations in the off-season. Cruise deals are better that time of year. And I think we should shorten the school day a bit. Teachers get really tired by the end of the day. We need a gate installed to make it safer for our teachers when they go to their cars . . ."

"Hold it, Henry!" Amy interjected. "Where on earth did you come up with that wish list?"

"As soon as you announced me as the new superintendent, staff members started calling. They gave me a lot of really great information, and I'm ready to get going on it!"

The board president took a deep breath. "Henry, let me give you a bit of advice. Slow down. Those changes are your goals, not those of the board. It's our job to tell the superintendent what the board wishes for the district to accomplish in the coming year. Then after we tell you what we want, you tell us how you are going to accomplish it. I am sure the board wants our attorney in the room for negotiations. I can guarantee you we won't agree to shorten the school day. And as for changing the calendar and spending money for a gated lot, well, it's just not going to happen!"

"I thought I was in charge, Amy!" sputtered the new superintendent.

(continued)

"You are," she responded. "You're in charge of staff. But hear me loud and clear, Henry. If you don't have the board's buy-in, this is not going to work. Everything needs to start with the board."

Discussion Questions

- How could the superintendent have better developed board support for achieving his goals?
- What steps should Henry take now?
- How should the superintendent manage the expectations of staff relative to changes they have asked him to make?

SETTING OBJECTIVES

One popular decision-making model is called SMART. SMART stands for:

- Specific
- Measurable
- Achievable
- Relevant
- Time Bound

It is not the purpose of this book to explore decision-making models in depth. One's local college or university likely has a course on designing organizational systems. The rationale for including this model is to make those wishing to become instructional leaders aware that if they and the board do not create goals that exhibit characteristics substantially similar to those developed under the aegis of SMART, it will be difficult to ascertain the efficacy of objectives and the attainability thereof.

"When an organization makes a concerted effort to call attention to and celebrate progress toward its goals, the commitments it demonstrates in day-to-day work, and the evidence of improved results, people within the organization are continually reminded of the priorities and what it takes to achieve them."—DuFour et al. (2006, p. 22)

One common goal of many school districts is to increase the level of achievement for students. That is a wonderfully intentioned sentiment. But what exactly does it mean? To one board member, it may mean winning awards for scholastic achievement. To another, it may mean increasing the number of graduates who are awarded four-year scholarships to college. The superintendent might interpret it as increasing reading scores on state achievement tests. Who is

> "Either play a leading role—hand in hand with your superintendent and senior administrators—in leading your district's innovation and change efforts, or sit on the sidelines, thereby not only missing a huge piece of the leadership action but also putting your district at risk of becoming the victim—rather than the leader—of change."—Eadie (2005, p. 50)

right? Because the goals are not specific, nobody really knows the real goal. No one can say if the goal is realistic, or if it is achievable, or even within what period the goal will be achieved.

Using the SMART model, goal statements must be Specific, Measurable, Achievable, Relevant, and Time Bound. From the original goal statement of "increasing the level of achievement for students," in order to comply within SMART, one can parse the objective and modify it to answer the questions:

"Increasing": By how much?

"The level of achievement": From what level to what level? In what subject areas?

"For students": Which students?

To be an effective and workable goal statement under SMART, it should also address the question "Over what time period"?

This is not to imply that there is a single correct answer to formulate goals using SMART objectives. One district might begin with a goal of "increasing the level of achievement for students" and decide to modify the objective to "increasing by 10 percent the base reading proficiency level of all fifth graders as measured by this year's state achievement test versus last year's result." Another district might take the same goal and decide to interpret it to mean "seeking to increase the number of high school seniors who are accepted into four-year colleges by 15 percent within the next three academic years."

Both districts began with the same goal of "increasing the level of achievement for students," but each district modified its goal into one that was Specific, Measurable, Achievable, Relevant, and Time Bound. Each goal was crafted to meet the specific needs of the district and the desires of the board, and each created a yardstick by which achievement could be measured. Absent objectives that are SMART, it is likely there will be too much "gray area" and not enough data by which actual progress can be accurately assessed.

FOCUS ON CORE VALUES

Once the strategic objectives of the school board have been determined, effective instructional leaders begin executing the tactics to implement the plan, first by sending clear messages to their principals, staff, and faculty.

> "When rules are contrary to what is best for kids, I am willing to say, 'This makes no sense. Let's focus on the kids.'"—Dr. Krista Parent, AASA National Superintendent of the Year, 2007

One example of putting a tactical plan into action effectively comes from Dr. Jack Gyves. He would often remind staff, "Don't expect me to come in and give plaudits just because the students are engaged. I don't confuse activity with achievement."

"There is a Portuguese saying," said another study participant. "'Some people move a lot just to keep warm.' We see these people. They are so busy, but they are not achieving a lot. You can dissect the difference between people who make things happen and those who just talk."

Instructional superintendents are advocates for directed action in the pursuit of building a better student practicum. They encourage and mentor their principals by emphasizing such things as time on task, minimizing disruptions, focusing on standards-based teaching, or simply weeding out superfluous activities unrelated to student education.

Dr. Dennis Fox gives an example of how he might encourage a behavioral change for teachers. "If teachers don't do effective pre-teaching, they are in for an uphill battle. So I would say, 'If you didn't start a lesson well, you'll need to meet with me.' I would tell them things I expect to see."

The core values of the governance team often focus on student achievement. "Kids first" was the statement most often made by superintendents who took part in this study. "Time and support for kids. That is my mantra. If given the time and support they need, they will learn," says Sandra Thorstenson.

"I have a sign on my desk: 'All decisions made in this office are made on behalf of students,'" says Henry Escobar.

Dr. Krista Parent, AASA National Superintendent of the Year for 2007, says, "Our core beliefs are: number one, children first, number two, all decisions are student centered, and number three, children learn best when they want to be at school; make it a great place to be. Guidelines and rules don't always support student achievement, so we change the rules in alignment with our core beliefs."

Clear expectations for teaching and learning begin with district leadership. The board determines the strategic objective. Superintendents decide on the tactics to achieve the board's goal, and the tactical plan is put into execution by the principals in the district.

One critical difference between superintendents who are instructional leaders and those who are merely maintaining the status quo is that educational leaders make inroads in student achievement by formulating district-wide tactical plans. Educational leaders can task principals throughout the district with a basic set of expectations for learning. These guidelines might include requirements that teachers check for understanding, that students can restate what they learned, and that effective pre-teaching is occurring.

Effective instructional leaders schedule time to be in classrooms every week, familiarizing themselves with what is being taught and how effectively instruction is being delivered. Instructional superintendents are not there to monitor. They focus on building collegial relationships with teachers and principals by discussing teaching strategies, auditing the teaching and learning processes, and reviewing data with teachers and principals.

When a superintendent has a firm sense of what is working in classrooms, one can effectively strategize how student educational experiences can improve by first analyzing how each decision will impact students. "They're all our kids" is the message that effective superintendents share with members of the school community. "That child belongs to every one of us. What we're doing in kindergarten will impact eighth grade," comments Renee Whitson.

> "What counts is not the number of hours you put in, but how much you put in the hours."—Anonymous (quote from Brady and Woodward 2005, p. 57)

Ned McNabb talks with school staff members about their impact on students. "My goal for everyone on campus, no matter what they do, is to see their number one job as education. I tell the grounds crew, 'You're there so kids learn. You're not there to mow the lawn. You're there to make every school a good place for kids.'"

McNabb says his philosophy resonates particularly well with classified employees. It demonstrates to every person in the school that their job has meaning, and proves the superintendent's respect for the role each employee plays in the educational process.

MENTOR INSTRUCTIONAL AND ADMINISTRATIVE LEADERSHIP

Top superintendents ensure their legacy by making it a priority to illuminate their passionate vision of the school or district's future to a core set of administrators in the district. One's assistant superintendents and cabinet in turn impart this attitude to their subordinates and teams. As an instructional leader mentors others, their desire to make a positive difference for students will iterate throughout the district.

> "I see my leadership as finding, leading, and supporting the critical few that give action to what we do."—Dr. Mimi Hennessey, a nine-year superintendent

Mentoring the district's leadership team produces a powerful formula for crafting a better educational experience for children. Instructional leaders must inculcate their assistants and cabinet members with the understanding that their most important work supports not only site principals, but also all those who work within the district. As with any pedagogy, coaching is both give and take. There is little place for control in the mentoring process. Effective mentoring requires all parties involved to set aside impediments to progress.

Henry Escobar is a strong proponent of making sure his leadership team has the tools it needs to get the job done. "At every meeting with my leadership team I say they need to leave with an ace. That ace might be an ignition of passion; it might be a key learning."

Effective superintendents spend significant time instructing, training, and coaching cabinet-level administrators and assistant superintendents, teaching those people to train others and disseminating knowledge throughout the school sites. Dr. Ron Leon explains, "It is all about our people. As superintendent you can't have every great idea. Our success comes from what the people in the organization do. Build people."

"Groom your management team. Set the expectation that this is a learning team. Set the bar as high as you can," instructs Gary Mekeel, a seventeen-year superintendent. Dr. Bill Mathis advises, "Hire very good people. Train them. Teach them well. Counsel and support when needed. Leave them alone otherwise."

The instructional superintendent is primarily an educator. "I tried to model teaching and learning everywhere I went," says Jim Brown.

Coaching, mentoring, teaching, and active learning on the part of the superintendent models the importance of these behaviors. "I pride myself in helping people to grow," avers Henry Escobar. "They grow until, like plants, they bloom and outgrow their pots. When you develop these people, you feel good about it. I pride myself in growing and teaching people."

By soliciting the opinions of others and requesting help in solving problems, the instructional superintendent can demonstrate to employees that their thoughts and experiences are valued. Dr. Louise Taylor says, "The rule: bring your brains. Rules are not the answer. They are only the information you need to craft the answer."

> "If you drop a frog into boiling water, it will instinctively jump out. But if you place a frog in a pot of cool water and then gradually increase the temperature, the frog won't notice that the water's getting hotter. It will sit there until the water boils—and will boil with it. The fate of that poached frog isn't so unlike that of some leaders who settle into routine or let small conveniences solidify into large habits—and allow inertia to set in."—Goleman et al. (2002, p. 126)

Before offering staff development and asking others to get behind an idea, it is important for the superintendent to fully understand the concepts she intends to teach. Says Dr. Jean Fuller, "I understand that if I am going to do this, I had better understand the ideas myself. They had better align with my goals and my staff. I make sure I embrace what is being taught to my people. Otherwise I don't offer it."

A district superintendent's approach to teaching and learning sends important messages. Instructional leaders impart to faculty and staff the concept that taking both a long-term view and a thoughtful approach to curriculum and instruction are necessary to create a high-functioning district.

Dr. Bill Mathis warns against jumping into training prematurely. "Please deliver us," he comments, "from people who attend a conference and come back and say, 'Now this is the way we must do things.'"

For the board's vision to take root, actions must first be examined from the perspective of their alignment with the district's stated

> "Enlist others in a common vision by appealing to their values, interests, hopes, and dreams."—Kouzes and Posner (1995, p. 148)

core values. If events are occurring in the district that are not aligned with, or that detract from, achieving the governance team's SMART goals, top instructional leaders take steps to immediately confront the issues and resolve them with celerity. "We have to selectively abandon things that are not contributing to our goal," says Becci Gillespie. One might choose to address issues on the spot, or one might instead facilitate change using staff development or training.

If an activity is perceived by the cabinet and assistants as being valued by the superintendent, it will be accorded much more consideration by the rest of the staff. The best district leaders agree, when a superintendent requires top leadership to attend training, the superintendent too should attend. "When I have something I want them to learn," says Sandra Thorstenson, "I attend the entire time. I am there all day in training. We learn together, and we read together."

> "Change moves more rapidly from innovator to innovator than from top down."—Dr. Joe Condon

Sometimes an integral element of effective instructional leadership is encouraging people not only to learn, but also to change their behavior. Susan Custer advises, "Attend and provide ongoing training. Learn along with them. Model to principals they can't just come to a workshop for ten minutes, grab a bagel, and leave."

Dr. Jack Gyves explains, "A change in behavior begins when cognitive dissonance is created. This dissonance is the distance between what we are doing and what we ought to be doing. In the absence of evidence to the contrary, people tend to think that what they are doing is really fine." It is the task of the instructional superintendent to create dissonance by asking the difficult questions. Exploring ideas and giving feedback help the leadership team members understand that what they are doing is not what they should be doing.

CONSTRUCT PRINCIPAL AND TEACHER LEADERSHIP

Superintendents who wish to be effective instructional leaders ensure that principals understand that they too are expected to be instructional leaders. Some principals believe that if they manage a school well, they are fulfilling their mandate. The finest instructional superintendents believe this to be untrue. They contend that a principal's primary task is to improve education for students by becoming instructional leaders themselves. Certainly, many managerial tasks take a principal's time. Principals who have inculcated the priorities of an instructional leader, however, put staff development at the top of their priority list and delegate some of the routine managerial tasks to others.

Part of the work of the instructional superintendent is in gearing education and training to help principals by filling gaps in their knowledge bases. One leader noted, "Educators know what they want, but not always what they need."

The superintendent who is an effective instructional leader must assume that principals will not enter the district with all the requisite skills for success. "Principals have different strengths," says Robert Hodges, a thirty-five-year educator and experienced superintendent. "We help guide them by creating our work together. Then they can take off with it. In that way, you have empowered that person to be an instructional leader. We keep them one step ahead."

Instructional leaders value classroom visits and being in the field to assess curriculum, faculty, and student learning. They should make clear that their expectations for principals are the same.

One can mentor principals to maintain high on-site visibility by walking the hallways as well as by conducting classroom visits. Days of the week when site administrators are expected to be in the classrooms can be designated, and one can make clear the expectation that, if top cabinet-level administrators visit the school, they will ordinarily expect to find a principal in a classroom and not in the office. Dr. Jack Gyves explains it this way: "It is not what you expect but what you inspect that gets done."

Some superintendents monitor sites by asking teachers when and how often they see the principal in their classrooms. Others ask principals to keep track of their class visits on a chart, which they review together during regular one-on-one meetings. Jack Gyves adds, "We changed the focus of the principal evaluation to: 'How are your kids doing? How do you know? Are you visiting classrooms?' If we ask teachers how often they [principals] have been observed and they haven't, the principal is in a deep swamp." He believes that instructional superintendents should remind principals, "All of the paperwork is peripheral to you doing your core job of working with teachers to improve instruction."

Superintendents who are instructional leaders understand the importance of using teaching time wisely and impress this knowledge on their principals. Good principals will demonstrate their mastery of this lesson by creating in their schools significant blocks of uninterrupted learning time and by prohibiting phone calls, assemblies, announcements, or other interruptions during academic time. "If it is not going to improve instruction, why are you doing it?" asks Dr. Dennis Fox.

Superintendents who place instructional leadership at the forefront of their work and principals who support those efforts can create a strong, solid educational program. Working together, the administration can focus on making student achievement the highest priority by creating a culture of continuous improvement throughout the district.

Occasionally principals are not as effective or as capable as the superintendent might wish. Regardless of a principal's shortcomings, it is always important to maintain the chain of command within the school site. Though superintendents have the power to march in and make changes, doing so undermines the structure of site-based leadership. One superintendent suggests that, in order to avoid usurping a principal's authority, site administrators should first be allowed to guide site remediation.

> "[Lincoln] created contagious enthusiasm among followers by demonstrating a sense of urgency toward attainment of his goals. He wanted them all to be like the dog in one of his favorite anecdotes: 'A man ... had a small bull-terrier that could whip all the dogs of the neighborhood. The owner of a large dog which the terrier had whipped asked the owner of the terrier how it happened that the terrier whipped every dog he encountered. "That," said the owner of the terrier, "is no mystery to me; your dog and the other dogs get half through a fight before they are ready; now, my dog is always mad!"'"—Quoted in Phillips (1992, p. 112)

An instructional leader's concern should not stop at the site administrator. It bears remembering that in every district there is significant instructional expertise. Teachers with years of experience and high levels of competence often are willing to become mentors for less-experienced or less-successful peers and should be encouraged to do so. "With teachers we say 'you are our experts.' We are going to focus our efforts on tapping into your expertise," says John Byerrum, former statewide Curriculum and Instruction Leader of the Year

Honoring the existing knowledge base within the district not only utilizes an available resource; it also demonstrates the value the organization places on existing staff members. While it is true that an outside speaker can sometimes be more effective in gaining attention for a particular change or innovation, it is also true that people learn well from peers they admire and respect. Giving seasoned teachers or those with particular instructional expertise the chance to shine before their peers makes them feel respected and valued; and their colleagues will benefit.

IMPLEMENT QUALITY-REVIEW PROGRAMS

Modifying the district teaching curriculum may sometimes be necessary because it has been demonstrated that the current educational program lacks depth, or that it has in some aspect proven to be unsatisfactory in promoting achievement of the district's academic goals.

When one contemplates adjusting the instructional offerings in the district, one ought to consider asking a small and enthusiastic group to pilot the change. Include the teachers' union in the decision, and coax people by asking their opinions. In making curriculum decisions, "Get agreement on the 'what,'" suggests Dr. Jack Gyves. "Involve teachers in the process. It is the province of the board and administration, but you must get the buy-in of opinion makers."

Once the pilot team has arrived at a decision, it is important to consider the curriculum modifications—what will be incorporated, as well as what teachers will no longer be asked to do. "Step back and see what we need to drop," suggests John Byerrum.

Any time there is an addition to the teaching day, effective instructional leaders should examine tasks they can release teachers from doing. Generally, it is best to permit schools to create fewer programs that allow for depth and breadth rather than to leave teachers scrambling to meet an overwhelming number of objectives. "My comment? Do less, deeper," says Dr. Joe Condon.

"Superintendents must understand that there are three levels of control: no control, remote control, and direct control," says Dr. Dennis Fox. "Remote control is the primary type of control a superintendent exerts. Direct control takes place in the classroom. If you are not teaching, you are exercising remote control." He asks, "How do you ensure that what you want to have happen there actually happens? You can increase the likelihood via relationships with the teacher and what happens in the classroom."

According to Dr. Fox, the question for the instructional leader becomes, "What can I do to increase the likelihood that my message will get out? I am ultimately responsible for what happens in classrooms in my district, and yet I have very little direct power to effect the most important changes." His conclusion is that superintendents must consistently communicate a philosophy of continuous improvement. "We should expect to see changed behavior. Every year, every adult must get a little better at the work they do."

Innovations are ephemeral unless there is institutional commitment to long-term change. "Really great superintendents, when their staff asks for or advocates for something, say, 'Is there evidence this will make a difference for teaching and learning?' Absent evidence to support the idea, the superintendent does not support it," explains Dr. Henry Mothner, director of the Division for School Improvement, Los Angeles County Office of Education.

If a district follows a new "hot trend" each year, faculty and administrators know they just have to wait a while and things will change yet again. If they don't like what is being implemented now, all they have to do is hold on, because something new is coming. Dr. Juli Quinn explains, "The history of sticking with an initiative tells people what to expect."

Discussion Scenario #12:
Instructional Leadership in Action

"The principal said he would cover my class so I can watch you teach the concepts of borrowing and carrying in math," chirped Jodi Schulz to her mentor teacher Kai Li.

"He does that a lot," said Kai. "Mr. Selkirk knows it helps when we learn from each other."

"Doesn't the principal have more important things to do than to cover a teacher's classes?"

"Is there anything more important than making sure we teach effectively?"

The novice teacher pondered the veteran instructor's response. Then she inquired, "Do you think he really reads all of those lesson plans we turn in each week?"

"He reads them, and he walks into our classrooms with them. He'll know what you're supposed to be teaching, and if he finds the kids coloring or watching a video instead of doing what you said they would be doing, you'll hear about it later," explained the mentor.

"Aren't there times when the kids are just tired or distracted? Sometimes they need an activity that isn't as difficult."

"Then take them outside and get some exercise," grinned Ms. Li. "It's OK to be doing an alternate activity, but if they're obviously just wasting time, or letting the kids waste time, that teacher will hear about it later from Mr. Selkirk."

Jodi thought for a moment. "Our principal has some high expectations for teachers," she said. "But along with that, he really supports us."

Kai nodded in agreement. "Mr. Selkirk will help us plan. He's taught classes when a teacher is sick, or upset, or maybe just needs a break. He and Dr. Smith, the district superintendent, are all about the kids. She'll probably be in your classroom several times this year, asking what you're doing and checking that the kids are working productively. Maybe she'll talk with you or the kids. She wants to be sure that we are all doing our best, for the kids, and as teachers."

"Isn't that sort of scary, having the superintendent visit?" asked Jodi, looking a bit unsettled.

Before she could receive an answer, she watched as the veteran teacher darted across the classroom and was quickly engrossed with one of her students, earnestly explaining how to carry the one to the tens column. Jodi smiled and moved nearer to better listen and learn from the skilled educator.

Discussion Questions

- What are your thoughts about a superintendent visiting classrooms?
- What would you identify as the core values of the principal and superintendent?
- Why is it important for the superintendent and principal to be attentive to instruction?

Effective superintendents break the cycle of endlessly embarking upon new initiatives by working with the board to determine what the district's core values are, then continuing with initiatives until the goals have been met. "The programs don't teach kids. Teachers teach kids," says Dr. Dennis Fox.

Working with staff to accept instructional change is different from allowing teachers to do whatever they want. "One of the biggest mistakes we make when we implement something is to let people opt out," advises Dr. Juli Quinn.

Principals can be understanding and listen to what the faculty has to say. However, it is important for instructional leaders to make clear their expectation that teachers, regardless of their personal feelings, will quickly and completely adopt the change.

CONCLUSION

The work of the superintendent affects the entire school system, but it ultimately has its greatest consequence in the classroom, where students feel the impact of instructional decisions and interventions made by district leadership. Effective instructional leaders predicate their core values on the students they serve. SMART decision making, making goals Specific, Measurable, Achievable, Relevant, and Time Bound, is a valuable methodology that can be used to set objectives, as well as a means by which to measure progress toward attaining them.

IMPLICATIONS FOR ACTION

- The board sets goals for the district, but optimally in partnership with the superintendent. Thoughtful, long-term approaches to curriculum and instruction are necessary from the top of the system to the classroom level.
- Consider using the SMART model of developing goals and evaluating progress. SMART is an acronym for Specific, Measurable, Achievable, Relevant, and Time Bound. If the goals a superintendent and a board create are not SMART, it is hard to ascertain if those goals have been achieved.
- Focus on mentoring and training the district's administrators. Building capacity by training school leaders is of critical importance to the success of the school system.
- Utilize the expertise of the staff to help mentor others.
- Develop a system that creates a culture of continuous improvement.
- Emphasize time on task.
- Minimize disruptions.
- Implement high-quality instructional programs. Once these programs are adopted, stay the course.
- Hold schools accountable. Visit classrooms and examine student learning.
- Remember that instructional leadership is the most important work of site principals and superintendents. Choose principals who are instructional leaders.

6

ASSESSMENT AND ACCOUNTABILITY

In God we trust. All others bring data.

—Sign in the office of Dr. Nancy Carroll

THE ASSESSMENT SYSTEM

Good leaders rely on data. They depend on it in order to make fact-based interpretations of student progress. Data comes in a variety of forms, from information gleaned from standardized testing to records gathered from classrooms throughout the district. In the words of Renee Whitson, regardless of the components of the assessment system, "Adults must be committed not by intentions but by the action of looking at data and doing something about it."

For an assessment system to work, test results must be reviewed at all levels of the system in order to make accurate assessments of where instructional strengths and weaknesses lie. That knowledge must then be communicated forthrightly to the board. A high-functioning board will review the information and work with the superintendent to formulate goals. An instructional superintendent will then transmit the new information throughout the district and develop the tactics to act upon it.

In the current climate of mandating achievement through legislation, it should not be surprising that the public has come to expect that student achievement scores will consistently rise. "You're either improving or you're declining. No matter what your scores are, even if you're at the top, if you drop, people will say, 'What's wrong?'" remarks Robert Hodges, a fourteen-year superintendent. "We have a responsibility to improve every year."

It is an unfortunate consequence of today's academic environment that teachers may help learners reach the level of achievement the law requires for their age cohort, only to be stymied by not knowing what to do to help students progress to the next level. "You feel like you are pushing the boulder up the hill and it is getting steeper and steeper," says Becci Gillespie, a superintendent with seven years of experience.

To best help students, an instructional leader must examine the goals set by the board and determine by what objective standards progress toward those goals can be measured. Maintaining incremental positive progress in the pursuit of achieving those aims is the principal function of any assessment system.

Creating an effective assessment begins with communicating the instructional leader's directive that there will be a district-wide approach to measuring student success and performance, and the superintendent's expectation to have these reviews supported, encouraged, and honored throughout the district. Conducting in-depth examinations and discussions of topics such as the proposed goal of testing, how the data will be generated, what will be measured, the means used to measure, and what the district hopes to learn from performing the assessment is necessary to building an effective system.

Analyzing data within a broad context can give a more complete sense of the experience of students in the system: their success and their challenges. "Part of the discussion has to be about benchmarks, attendance data, and discipline in addition to other measures," explains Susan Custer.

Clearly defining the scope of what data is to be used, as well as describing how and why, will help to guide staff in making their best and most accurate interpretations of what testing results indicate. Creating distinct and unambiguous objectives allows faculty and principals to use a set of predetermined heuristics to create a framework within which they can best use the information to guide instruction. "If you're asking who is learning and who is not, you can't just find out at the end of the year on the state test," says Renee Whitson.

Dr. Dennis Fox also encourages instructional leaders to look at the data from a variety of perspectives. He advises, "Look at the same kids, the same test, the same time, but through a different lens."

No matter how the numbers are deconstructed, it is important for an effective instructional leader to discuss with faculty and principals areas of curricular strength for the students versus those areas of apparent weakness. Knowing the benchmarks the district wants to track and developing ways to accurately measure results is essential, because rigorous analysis of detailed data can often yield unexpected results. "Our people are very data driven. We don't do 'I think' or 'I believe.' We use data to guide instruction," explains twelve-year veteran superintendent Dr. Nancy Carroll.

What should instructional leaders do with the data that is collected? "We have data teams," counsels Sandra Thorstenson. "They are made of different people and have a different emphasis each year. One year we might study English learners, the next math, literacy, or special education. Every month these data groups get together to examine the information they have gathered. They conduct focus groups. At the end of the year, these teams come up with recommendations."

Dr. Rene Townsend advises superintendents to do more than just review test results. "Bring data in [and ask] what does this tell us? Have trust. Use inquiry. Allow your people to come up with answers. Trust them. Collaborate. Everyone wants collaboration. They want to be honored for what they know. They want to be better. Get into why people wanted to be teachers in the first place."

Using the "data team approach" like the one Thorstenson advocates can help district leaders achieve multiple goals. The key to effective use of this methodology is to engage a wide array of people from throughout the school system in conversations about the data.

Differing perspectives from educators in diverse disciplines allows a variety of input concerning whatever specific data points you wish to examine.

The data team approach emphasizes creating a holistic assessment focused on specific needs and allows for concomitant staff development activities to be developed based on those needs. Renee Whitson describes how this process works in her district. "We look at data. After we get the data, we come together in job-alike groups. We collaborate about how kids are doing. We compare interventions. We don't have a one-size-fits-all intervention."

The critical work is based on what student data is telling the team, Whitson continues. "We take a structured look at power standards at the grade level and identify two to four students in the next six weeks that need interventions in each classroom. We provide help before and after school for these students. If we are looking at data and students aren't moving forward, we are going to look at their programs."

"We are arguing that opportunity to learn must move beyond the question of 'Was it taught?' to the far more important question of 'Was it learned?' If the answer to that question is no for some students, then the school must be prepared to provide additional opportunities to learn during the regular school day in ways that students perceive as helpful rather than punitive."
—DuFour et al. (2006, p. 77)

Data analysis must be done thoroughly. Susan Custer says, "You must understand the background reasons for problems and refer to them alongside the data. Based on that information, you then ask, 'As a result of what we know, what will we now do?'"

BUILDING A CULTURE OF CONTINUOUS IMPROVEMENT

Effective superintendents build a culture of continuous improvement by putting systems in place that enable positive change to occur. "There is only one main thing: building a culture of continuous improvement in student achievement. Period," says Dr. Dennis Fox.

Jim Brown, who after a twenty-seven-year career as a superintendent of schools now mentors other superintendents, agrees. "You must have systems, structures, and processes for the use of data. Reviewing data is like getting your daily exercise. You can't just do it when you feel like it. Data must become a part of your regimen, what you do as an organization to continuously improve."

> "When you are the leader and you want people to speak in terms of performance, you must model the interpretation of the data you want them to emulate."—Susan Custer

Dr. Henry Mothner, director of the Division for School Improvement at the Los Angeles County Office of Education, oversees a division that specializes in addressing the needs of low-performing schools and school districts. Mothner explains, "All components of the system are interlinked or woven together. The tapestry is all about improving achievement. All systems are tied to 'what differences will this make for student achievement?'"

It is the role of the superintendent to create a sustainable system for student achievement. Once it is in place, it becomes the superintendent's responsibility to ensure its continuous improvement. Instructional leaders must train educators to become skilled at the study of student data.

> "We can just become overwhelmed with data. We can analyze it many ways, but unless you're going to do something about it, how can it translate into improvement in reading and learning? There must be next steps in the process."—Dr. Krista Parent, 2007 AASA National Teacher of the Year

Not many people are inherently talented at assessing student work: compiling data, paring it down to manageable information, interpreting it, and sending it back through the system to positively impact instruction. There are many consulting agencies available to help either by disaggregating the data, or by facilitating instructional courses designed to teach educators to do it themselves. Regardless of how one chooses to break the data down, there is no substitute for a rigorous analysis of the information. The numbers ought to be closely scrutinized by those who work directly with students and those who oversee them.

Building a culture of continuous improvement is important, and a system for gathering and analyzing data helps to ensure that the process one hopes to create or improve is one that needs to be built or bettered. Measuring student outcomes can confirm that teaching methodologies are conducive to student learning. Regardless of the structure, Jim Brown reminds instructional leaders to "be very heavily data driven. Use clear, measurable goals and have indicators in place that tell you how you met those goals. Use benchmarks . . . Compare your district to others."

"Align instruction with content standards and tests. Don't teach a person to swim and then test them on basketball."—Dr. James Phares, AASA Superintendent of the Year National Finalist, 2008

Data is important, but it does not form in a vacuum. Numbers are contextual, though they can be parsed and analyzed in almost infinite ways. One must work to ensure that numbers are examined within their proper framework. Without understanding the "numbers behind the numbers," attempting improvements throughout the system might ignore the students most in need of intervention and assistance.

Dr. Dennis Fox says, "Use data as a guide to decision making. Look at it not just from a need to interpret. Draw inferences. Look at data and trends across the district. Is there evidence that we're getting more effective with this group of kids? Now look at individual schools. Do some schools appear more successful? Is there evidence that one grade level has made more progress? Is there evidence that if we continue to do what we are doing, we should expect different results?"

MAINTAINING A SYSTEM OF INTERNAL ACCOUNTABILITY

Along with building systems to gather and analyze data, and then putting that information to work in schools, effective superintendents must also create systems of internal accountability in order to positively impact student achievement. Dr. Dennis Fox suggests, "We can't wait for end-of-year scores . . . we must have our own system. The principal needs to hold the teacher accountable, and the superintendent needs to hold the principal accountable for what we are doing that is less than satisfactory."

> "Hope is not a strategy."—Dr. Dennis Fox

It is the job of the superintendent to set up a structure to ensure that what is expected will be taught, what is taught will be measured, what is measured will be studied, and that the results will be considered when determining the next phase of teaching. As Dr. Fox asks, "If a superintendent believes something is key to teaching and learning, how do they ensure this is transferred to the classroom?" The answer is to maintain accountability throughout the system.

Superintendents must ensure that ongoing data gathering and analysis is occurring in the district. In addition to benchmark testing, new data must be consistently examined and assessed so change can occur as a result. Effective superintendents set up systems that require teachers to continuously improve at the job of teaching, and they judge improvement not on a gut feeling, but on the test scores that reflect what the students are learning.

> "No longer can a superintendent go before the school board or media and simply claim that the district is doing a great job in educating students. Superintendents must have the skills to explain how well the students compare to others in the state and nation. The new school executive must be an authority in monitoring and evaluating student achievement on the basis of objectives and expected student outcomes."
> —Hoyle et al. (2005, p. 23)

Fox explains how system accountability might work. "To what extent do you actually discuss the results of benchmark exams? Who holds teachers accountable for these discussions? You do not get system-wide results unless the superintendent holds the principal accountable. A superintendent might, for example, tell principals there is going to be a testing week. After the test, you are going to come in and tell me what you've learned from this. I want to know what happened on the test and what you as a principal are doing to ensure that teachers are making changes to their instructional practices based on these results. If the superintendent doesn't have that expectation for principals, why would the principals have it for teachers?"

After this conversation, says Fox, the superintendent might ask, "If I go to your school in the next six weeks, what would I expect to see your teachers doing differently?" He reminds us, however, "There will be lag time between a change in adult behavior and an improvement in the results of student learning."

CONCLUSION

Creating systems and frameworks for collecting, contextually analyzing, and applying data is where the art of teaching and the science of measuring results meld together. The resulting amalgamation of the two disciplines yields the single best method to measure the impact of a district's effort in student attainment of specified learning goals.

Teaching without testing is like spending without balancing one's checkbook; there can be unanticipated consequences. Taking the time to examine the outcomes of the district's teaching and learning process provides critical information to the administration as well as to the teacher. Drawing accurate conclusions and employing methods based on the findings will positively impact the ultimate success of the school district. Ensuring accountability throughout the system makes all parties stakeholders in the support and maintenance of a cycle of continuous improvement.

IMPLICATIONS FOR ACTION

- Leaders must remain committed to gathering and assessing data, and to basing decisions on logical inferences drawn from the analysis of the data.

- One should communicate that student and teacher assessments are system-wide expectations that must be supported, encouraged, expected, and honored.
- "There is only one main thing: building a culture of continuous improvement in student achievement. Period." (Dr. Dennis Fox)
- All systems must be unalterably focused on positively answering the question "How will this make a difference in student achievement?"
- It is the instructional superintendent's role to create and implement systems for assessing academic achievement, creating a culture of continuous improvement, and ensuring internal accountability.

7

EQUITY

People get caught up—they try to be fair and equal. That's wrong. Fair is how people need to be treated based on a circumstance or situation. Equal is equal. Those are two different things. You have to balance the two.

—Dr. James Phares, AASA Superintendent
of the Year National Finalist, 2008

BUILD AWARENESS OF ISSUES RELATED TO EQUITY

In Charles Dickens's *A Christmas Carol*, the Ghost of Christmas Present and the tight-pocketed Ebenezer Scrooge gaze at the figures of two ragged children. The ghost cautions, "This boy is Ignorance. This girl is Want. Beware them both, and all of their degree, but most of all beware this boy, for on his brow I see that written which is Doom, unless the writing be erased."

As in Dickens's classic, while Want might be unfortunate, Ignorance spells doom. Children are in need of instructional leaders who will make it their mission to eliminate the barriers erected by economic disadvantage. Instructional leaders must face the same frightful torments the ghost revealed to Scrooge.

Every person possesses a measure of power he can use to remove the frightening visages of ignorance and want. The opportunity to begin to sever poverty's ties to low achievement lies within every district's grasp. The question remains in this day as it did then: We see what needs to be done. Who among us has the courage to act? Effective instructional leaders must examine for themselves ways in which they can give their time, resources, and attention to ameliorate the struggles of their most needy students.

There is an achievement gap in many school districts across the United States. This gap is defined as the disparity between the achievements of a child of one racial or economic group versus that of other students not in that group. In order to lead effectively on this issue, one must recognize the moral imperative to change the system. It is up to the instructional superintendent to redefine achievement in terms of educational equity.

> "If you believe they can't learn, then all we're doing is child care. What if hospitals believed 20, 30 percent of the patients would not make it? Would you go there?"—Ken Noonan, thirty-year superintendent and former president, California State Board of Education

In order to address the issue, an effective instructional leader must first rethink and redefine the achievement gap. Bridging any type of equity gap will not be easy. It requires reconsidering the traditional model of student achievement. Consider framing the definition of "achievement gap" as the interval existing between a child's achievement level and the educational system's ability to best meet that child's individual needs.

Effective instructional school leaders must change from a deficit frame of mind to one of abundance. One can reconsider the statement "If a child can't accomplish a task, there is a problem with this child" and instead redefine achievement in equity terms and ask the question differently: "If there is a gap between what we are teaching and what this child is learning, what can we do differently?" Dr. Dennis Fox stresses the importance of differentiating the questions, and of creating new and alternative outcomes. He warns, "We have no reason to think things will improve unless the adults are doing something differently."

Poverty poses significant barriers to academic success in terms of individual student achievement, as well as for an entire school district. "Children don't learn if they're hungry. They don't learn if they have a toothache. They don't learn if they have to sleep in the cab of their mom's truck. Some educators understand that. Some don't," laments Dr. Bill Mathis.

> "How do we frame a conversation about this so our country's story has a happy ending? Because if it doesn't work for some of us, it can't work for any of us."—Cambron-McCabe et al. (2005, p. 147)

Children who come to school lacking basic food and warm clothing, language skills, or experiences that are shared or similar to those in their peer group often begin their educational experiences perceived as laggards. As they move through the school system, rather than catching up, these young people tend to lag further behind. Equity can only be achieved when an instructional leader makes it a district priority to develop new systems and methods to ameliorate the shortfalls in satisfying those children's needs. There must be an institutional commitment to change, not an acceptance of the status quo.

All but the most fortunate school systems grapple with the issues of poverty and educational inequity. Districts can offer breakfast and lunch, immunization clinics, or other social programs that address a child's physical needs, but they often fail to meet a child's educational needs. Those needs can be met only by having teachers in the classroom who are sensitized to the nature of the gaps between what their students are capable of achieving and their current level of performance.

USE DATA TO IDENTIFY THE ACHIEVEMENT GAP

District leaders may intuitively feel there is a wide variation in achievement between students with similar abilities. But unless the problem is accurately measured and quantified, no effective solution can be created. Jim Brown uses inquiry to discuss student achievement. "Which students in this school are below grade level? What is the game plan for them? If we weren't getting enough progress in an area, what different approaches do we need to have in that area?"

Brown says that while he was superintendent, "I sent a note to the principal: 'I want to see the names of every student in your school that has not been reclassified [from English learner to fluent speaker] in a five-year period and the plan for their learning.' [After doing so,] I started to see more reclassifications coming in."

Looking only at standardized test scores is not enough. Analyzing multiple data points from a variety of perspectives allows one to uncover patterns or deficits in teaching methods that might previously go unnoticed. Examining disparate data ranging from discipline and attendance records to scores on annual tests for English learners, and augmenting these with scores from frequent benchmark examinations, can provide new windows through which we can see gaps in the system.

> "Let the data do the talking. You lead by listening and following, then move the agenda forward."—Manny Barbara

ENCOURAGE COURAGEOUS CONVERSATIONS

Holding conversations about the impact of poverty and gaps in student achievement is a first step in identifying some of the most significant needs of students. Discussions about inequity are quite often uncomfortable and daunting. They force participants to confront the unfortunate fact that the system is falling short in meeting the needs of some students. Achievement concerns often occur where most school

> "Equity work is very intense. It is hard for people. We have to build the capacity of people to handle the courageous conversations." —Manny Barbara

systems need the most help: along the lines of race, gender, and economic background. Effective instructional superintendents consider addressing these issues a core component of their work.

Some top superintendents step courageously forward to address issues of equity. They meet with the various ethnic groups that comprise their districts and initiate what has been previously referred to as an "uncomfortable conversation." They believe that directly speaking about race and economic factors with those who are most impacted by them is the most effective means to learn specific ways to better meet a student population's needs.

> "Race and class are areas where you can't succeed by making it up as you go along."—Cambron-McCabe et al. (2005, p. 155)

Manny Barbara describes his reasons for holding "uncomfortable conversations" in his community: "We must include people of different ethnicities in these conversations, recognizing they may see our systems through a completely different lens than we do. We must ease into the equity conversation. We developed a 'closing the achievement gap plan of action' that involved parents, staff, and the leadership team. I met with African American parents and said, 'What can we do to get you more involved?' I heard things that were hurtful to hear. I heard 'we don't want to be invisible at the school sites. We want books with people that look like us.'"

A common concern is how best to begin a conversation with parents whose children are not succeeding in the school system. Top instructional superintendents often advise that the best way to begin is by showing parents how their ethnic group is achieving in comparison with others, and then asking them what they believe the school system can do to help bridge the gap.

> "Trust that meaningful conversations can change your world."—Margaret Wheatley, Turning to One Another: Simple Conversations to Restore Hope to the Future (quoted in Cambron-McCabe et al. 2005, p. 181)

Jim Brown suggests, "Use data to talk a lot about who is and who is not making it, then ask, 'What is our responsibility to make this situation better?'"

Discussion Scenario #13: Courageous Conversations

"The parents are going to thank you for asking about the achievement gap," said the PTA president before the meeting. "Count on it."

"This isn't going to be easy," thought Dr. Ralph Smith as he cleared his throat. It was his first meeting with an African American parent group. "In our district, non-native English learners are doing better than our African American students. How am I going to broach this topic with parents without parents thinking I am blaming them or their children for their child's difficulties?" Despite his discomfort, Superintendent Smith began. "I asked you to come today because we are looking for ways in which our schools can better meet your children's needs. Let's take a look at what the numbers are telling us is happening in our schools."

As they listened to the analysis of the data, the parents reacted with palpable concern. "We want to help our children, but sometimes the homework is just too much. By the time we get home from our jobs and put dinner on the table, it's late," cried one parent. Echoed a second, "There's just so much. By the time we sit down at night, my kid is exhausted, and her homework becomes a shouting match or she just ends up getting frustrated."

The discussion ranged into the night, and other comments resonated with the superintendent. "It isn't just homework. My wife wants to volunteer in the classroom, but when she did, the teachers acted like it was a bother to gather things for her to do."

"We don't see people who look like us in the school building, in the textbooks, or in the artwork in the hallway."

"How is my child supposed to come to believe that people like him can achieve when there are no examples for him?"

Despite the nature of the uncomfortable conversation, the parents were as thoughtful and respectful to each other as they were to Dr. Smith. At the end of the meeting, he thanked them for their feedback. "This is only the beginning," the superintendent told them. "We have a great deal of work to do. If we are going to close the achievement gap, I'm going to need all of your help."

As the parents were filtering out, a father made his way to the front of the room and clasped the district leader on the arm. "Thank you, Dr. Smith. It is good to know you want to help, and all I want is for my daughter to do well." It was a discussion that was difficult to begin and uncomfortable to take part in, but the district leader thought that the district was already making great strides toward a productive future.

Discussion Questions

- Why were the parents receptive to holding a conversation about the academic problems of only African American children?
- Is holding conversations with small groups of parents appropriate work for the superintendent? Why or why not?
- If one wished to meet with a group of parents from a minority ethnic group to discuss areas of academic concern to their children, how might one best initiate the conversation?

Conversations about educational equity are often uncomfortable for several reasons. They force superintendents to admit that they do not have all the answers when it comes to meeting the needs of poor and minority students. Uncomfortable conversations require discussing issues that may be unique to a single ethnic group. And when one takes the time to contemplate the world, one sometimes feels compelled to ponder such disturbing questions as "Did I do my best for the child that needed my help the most?"

Superintendents who initiate uncomfortable conversations can learn many things merely by making a respectful effort to listen to parents whose children are struggling. Information gathered in situations conducive to holding rich and honest dialogues between instructional leaders and parents, however awkward or uncomfortable initiating those conversations may be, can begin the process of closing a district's achievement gap. Conversations about equity, and making decisions to correct problems based on what one learns from them, are ways to ensure that the important work of the district is being accomplished.

CHANGE TEACHING METHODS

Effective instructional leaders can only control their approach to teaching and learning in their attempt to narrow the achievement gap. The pedagogies currently used in a district may not be geared to the ways in which specific students need to learn. In other words, it may be that administrators and faculty come to school underprepared for the students, and not the converse. There may be a fundamental mismatch between the background and training of educators and the students they serve.

> "The future of the public schools will be determined by how well we educate the changing clientele."
> —Dr. Jack Gyves

One's thoughts are filtered through a prism that reflects one's experiences. Accordingly, when students are not succeeding, it is not unusual for an administrator to think the problem is not with the system, but with the student. "We must keep telling teachers that it is not up to the kids to change; it is up to the teachers to change," counsels Dr. Jack Gyves. Says one superintendent, "Poor and minority students do poorly because we don't teach them well, not because they're poor and minority. It is our responsibility. What it depends on is teachers and classrooms. Poor and minority kids can do this. We just have to show them it can be done."

> "Most children start life equally equipped to learn and grow. Preventing an achievement gap from developing is likely to be easier than fixing it after the fact." —Cambron-McCabe et al. (2005, p. 172)

CHANGE HOW EMPLOYEES ARE RECRUITED

Effective superintendents strategize about how to attract the best teachers to the lowest-performing schools. Students who are the best prepared for school are commonly most attractive to teachers; those who are least prepared and harder to teach are less so. This means the students who most need the most experienced teachers tend not to get them.

As teachers gain in experience and expertise, their propensity is to queue for openings at schools serving wealthier or higher-achieving students, leaving open positions at schools serving minorities, the poor and the underprivileged. In many school districts, it is not uncommon to find the average years of teaching experience at high-achieving schools

> "Remember you serve the social good. Not business. Not test makers. You build a better society. That's why we're in the business."—Dr. Bill Mathis

much greater than those of teachers in schools serving students from backgrounds of poverty.

Educational leaders can take steps to reinvent this system by developing programs and incentives to attract the best teachers to schools where students need them most. The educational system is highly resistant to this change. There seems to be almost a "right" of veteran teachers to teach certain grades and hold positions in some schools. These are the types of situations in which the superintendent should ask difficult questions. Where is the focus of the district? Is the work about student achievement, or is it about teacher comfort? The educational system cannot have it both ways. Either the best teachers begin working with the students who most need them, or the achievement gap will continue.

RECOGNIZE TEACHER HEROES

Most school districts have a small but strong cadre of "teacher heroes." They are a core group of excellent teachers who make it their work to do the very best they can for the students who need them the most. These educators seek out schools with high minority or low-income populations and make an honest effort to make a difference for these students. Teacher heroes come to school every day ready to go the extra mile to determine their students' unmet needs and to make every effort to close the equity and achievement gap.

"Effective superintendents find ways to help and honor those who are doing the hard work it takes to move the students forward. We need to recognize in a public way the people who are making a dent in this," says Jim Brown.

There are various methods in which school districts reward excellent teaching in struggling schools. Some districts offer teachers with extensive years of experience the opportunity to obtain credit for all of their teaching years when they agree to work at the highest-poverty schools in the district. Besides structural incentives, making it a point to thank and honor teacher heroes helps create a desire to assist students who need them the most. Sometimes a simple "thank you" or a handwritten note expressing thanks for hard work is all it takes to make a teacher feel appreciated, wanted, and committed.

BUILD SYSTEMS TO CLOSE THE ACHIEVEMENT GAP

Issues of equity are some of the more complex and difficult concerns for instructional superintendents. "We have a great opportunity in public education to impact the lives of kids. There is a moral obligation we have to address the gap," says Dr. Kent Bechler.

Addressing and redressing equity issues have to be top priorities for every superintendent. Frequent opportunities to correct issues of equity occur in a superintendent's day-to-day work, and decisions ought to be driven by a mission to improve the situation for students of poverty. "In dealing with poverty, equal results require unequal distribution of resources," says Jim Brown.

"Don't depend on other things. Depend on yourself. You are the hope."—Ken Noonan

Instructional leaders can either use "closing the achievement gap" as a goal and frame of reference and give more in time and resources to schools that need the help most, or they can continue to do business as it has always been done. Those who choose to be instructional leaders understand they can make a significant difference in the lives of students, parents, and the community. Administrators who excel as instructional leaders do not conceive of addressing equity issues as a part of their job. They see it as an integral and inherent obligation of their profession.

CONCLUSION

Students from poverty and those from minority racial, linguistic, and ethnic backgrounds bring complex needs to school each day. Strong school systems provide an equitable learning experience for all students. Exceptional instructional superintendents take the time to speak with parents of socioeconomically disadvantaged and minority students to learn more about the specific needs of their student population. They share data with the parents, explain its implications, and encourage parental feedback and involvement in their child's education.

An instructional leader must encourage teacher heroes to continue their efforts in the classroom. Top superintendents find innovative ways to fulfill their obligations to students, the community, the board, and their profession. They align resources and teaching staff, and construct systems and schools intended to meet the needs of all students, from those who excel to those in greatest need.

IMPLICATIONS FOR ACTION

- "Achievement gap" can be defined as the disparity between the achievements of a child of one racial or economic group versus that of other students not in that group.
- The equity gap can be closed by changing from a deficit frame of mind to one of abundance.
- Consider achievement gaps to be the problem of the school system, rather than assuming that the student has a deficit.
- Have the courage to hold uncomfortable conversations about issues of poverty, race, and ethnicity.

- Analyze data. Look closely at what it says about the achievement of minority groups within the school system. Use the analysis as a springboard for conversations from a model of inquiry rather than with an eye to the deficits in achievement in these students.
- Create incentives to attract experienced, high-quality teachers to the schools that need them the most.
- Applaud "teacher heroes," those faculty members whose personal mission is to serve poor and minority students.
- Addressing issues of equity is an important and inherent obligation of an effective instructional leader.

CONCLUSION

There is no role more important to the superintendency than that of creating systems that support instructional success. This book has been crafted as a guide for superintendents to refer to as they move along the path of instructional improvement.

Superintendents who choose to become instructional leaders can make a tremendous difference in achievement for the many students they serve. They understand the importance of making the various elements of the district's educational system work to every student's advantage.

Building a strong governance team and choosing personnel wisely are essential elements of a successful superintendency. Instructional leaders communicate the district's core values, share educational objectives, and mentor staff and assistant superintendents. Creating systems of gathering, measuring,

> "There is only one main thing: building a culture of continuous improvement in student achievement. Period."—Dr. Dennis Fox

and using data, fostering a culture of continuous improvement and internal accountability, and attempting to address equity issues further separate the top instructional leaders in the field.

Using this book as a guide, one can "stand in the classroom and look back up the system," as Dr. Juli Quinn suggests. Applying the lessons within will help superintendents become better instructional leaders and aid them in the creation of a sustainable educational system that promotes high-quality instruction, student achievement, and equity for all.

BIBLIOGRAPHY

Bogue, E. Grady (2010). *Leadership Legacy Moments: Visions and Values for Stewards of Collegiate Mission.* Lanham, MD: Rowman & Littlefield Education.

Brady, C., and O. Woodward (2005). *Launching a Leadership Revolution: Mastering the Five Levels of Influence.* Boston: Business Plus.

Cambron-McCabe, N., L. L. Cunningham, J. Harvey, and R. H. Koff (2005). *The Superintendent's Field Book: A Guide for Leaders of Learning.* Thousand Oaks, CA: AASA and Corwin Press.

Cashman, K. (1998). *Leadership from the Inside Out: Becoming a Leader for Life.* Minneapolis, MN: TCLG.

Collins, J. (2001). *Good to Great: Why Some Companies Make the Leap ... and Others Don't.* New York: Harper Business.

Cramer, K., and H. Wasiak (2006). *Change the Way You See Everything through Asset-Based Thinking.* Philadelphia: Running Press.

Deneen, James (2009). *Schools That Succeed, Students Who Achieve: Profiles of Programs Helping All Students to Learn.* Lanham, MD: Rowman & Littlefield Education.

DuFour, Richard, Rebecca DuFour, R. Eaker, and T. Many (2006). *Learning by Doing: A Handbook for Professional Learning Communities at Work™.* Bloomington, IN: Solution Tree.

Eadie, D. (2005). *Five Habits of High-Impact School Boards.* Lanham, MD: Scarecrow Education.

George, B., and P. Sims (2007). *True North: Discover Your Authentic Leadership*. San Francisco: John Wiley & Sons.

Goleman, D., R. Boyatzis, and A. McKee (2002). *Primal Leadership: Learning to Lead with Emotional Intelligence*. Boston: Harvard Business School Press.

Gordon, R., T. J. Kane, and D. O. Staiger (2006). *Identifying Effective Teachers Using Performance on the Job*. Washington, DC: Hamilton Project, the Brookings Institute.

Hettleman, Kalman R. (2009). *It's the Classroom, Stupid: A Plan to Save America's Schoolchildren*. Lanham, MD: Rowman & Littlefield Education.

Hoyle, J. R., L. G. Björk, V. Collier, and T. Glass (2005). *The Superintendent as CEO*. Thousand Oaks, CA: Corwin Press.

Hutchison, Charles B., ed. (2009). *What Happens When Students Are in the Minority: Experiences and Behaviors That Impact Human Performance*. Lanham, MD: Rowman & Littlefield Education.

Johnston, G. L., G. E. Gross, R. S. Townsend, P. Lynch, P. B. Novotney, B. Roberts, L. Garcy, and L. Gil (2002). *Eight at the Top: A View Inside Public Education*. Lanham, MD: Scarecrow Press.

Kouzes, J. M., and Barry Z. Posner (1995). *The Leadership Challenge: How to Keep Getting Extraordinary Things Done in Organizations*. San Francisco: Jossey-Bass.

Kriegel, R., and D. Brandt (1997). *Sacred Cows Make the Best Burgers: Developing Change-Ready People and Organizations*. New York: Warner Business Books.

Lencioni, P. (2005). *Overcoming the Five Dysfunctions of a Team: A Field Guide for Leaders, Managers, and Facilitators*. San Francisco: Jossey-Bass.

Lytle, James H. (2010). *Working for Kids: Educational Leadership as Inquiry and Invention*. Lanham, MD: Rowman & Littlefield Education.

Manley, Robert J., and Richard J. Hawkins (2009). *Designing School Systems for All Students: A Toolbox to Fix America's Schools*. Lanham, MD: Rowman & Littlefield Education.

Maxwell, J. C. (1998). *The 21 Irrefutable Laws of Leadership: Follow Them and People Will Follow You*. Nashville, TN: Thomas Nelson.

——. (1999). *The 21 Indispensable Qualities of a Leader: Becoming the Person Others Will Want to Follow*. Nashville, TN: Thomas Nelson.

McEwan, E. K. (2003). *Ten Traits of Highly Effective Principals: From Good to Great Performance*. Thousand Oaks, CA: Corwin Press.

Pepper, Matthew J., T. D. London, Mike L. Dishman, and Jessica L. Lewis (2010). *Leading Schools during Crisis: What School Administrators Must Know.* Lanham, MD: Rowman & Littlefield Education.

Phillips, D. (1992). *Lincoln on Leadership: Executive Strategies for Tough Times.* New York: Warner Books.

Reeves, D. B. (2006). *The Learning Leader: How to Focus School Improvement for Better Results.* Alexandria, VA: Association for Supervision and Curriculum Development.

Scott, S. (2002). *Fierce Conversations: Achieving Success at Work & in Life, One Conversation at a Time.* New York: Berkley Books.

Townsend, R. S., J. R. Brown, and W. L. Buster (2005). *A Practical Guide to Effective School Board Meetings.* Thousand Oaks, CA: Corwin Press.

Townsend, R. S., G. L. Johnson, G. E. Gross, P. Lynch, L. Garcy, B. Roberts, and P. B. Novotney (2007). *Effective Superintendent–School Board Practices: Strategies for Developing and Maintaining Good Relationships With Your Board.* Thousand Oaks, CA: Corwin Press.

Wagner, T., R. Kegan, L. Lahey, R. W. Lemons, J. Garnier, D. Helsing, A. Howell, and H. T. Rasmussen (2006). *Change Leadership: A Practical Guide to Transforming Our Schools.* San Francisco: John Wiley & Sons.

ABOUT THE AUTHOR AND PARTICIPANTS

Linda K. Wagner is a credentialed teacher and administrator with over twenty-two years of experience in the field of education, the last seven as a superintendent. She was named 2009 Superintendent of the Year for the Association of California School Administrators, Region 15. She earned her master's degree in educational administration and her doctorate in educational leadership at the University of LaVerne (California).

*

John Aycock has been a superintendent for over sixteen years. In 2007 he was honored by his peers as Superintendent of the Year for his region. He currently serves 13,000 K–12 students and 1,100 adults.

Ralph Baker has received numerous awards over his twenty-eight-year career, including the National Quality Superintendent of the Year Award from the Center for Schools of Quality. He presently serves 12,000 students.

Manny Barbara has received numerous awards, including Superintendent of the Year for his region. He has been a superintendent for over ten years. Mr. Barbara presents at workshops and symposiums for state and local educators.

Dr. Kent Bechler is the superintendent of the tenth-largest school district in California, with a population of over 51,000 students. His academic work includes teaching adjunct classes at the university level and consulting.

John Beck has been a superintendent for over fourteen years. He was named Tulare County Administrator of the Year in 1997 and was awarded Superintendent of the Year 2002 by the Association of California School Administrators, Region 11.

Richard Bray serves 21,000 K–12 students in Southern California. He has held a variety of state-level positions, including liaison to the California Board of Education and the No Child Left Behind Task Force.

Jim Brown currently teaches and mentors superintendents, following a twenty-seven-year career as a superintendent of schools. He has received many awards but believes his greatest accomplishment was in maintaining a focus on teaching and learning.

Noel J. Buehler has spent the past eleven years as a superintendent. He received the Sonoma County Administrator of the Year Award in 2006 and the Association of California School Administrators (ACSA) Award for Regional Superintendent in 2007.

John Byerrum has been honored as statewide Curriculum and Instruction Leader of the Year, Superintendent of the Year, and Administrator of the Year. He is active in community organizations and has been a superintendent for over fifteen years.

Dr. Magdalena Carrillo-Mejia served as the superintendent for one of California's largest school districts. Her perspectives concerning a large district team's role in school site visits contributed helpful information to this book.

Dr. Nancy Carroll has been a superintendent since 1996. She is bilingual and has extensive experience working with English learners in a variety of capacities.

Dr. Joseph Condon is a longtime superintendent. He was recognized in *Leading with Soul* by Lee Bolman and Terrence Deal and counts among his numerous accolades the Pepperdine Superintendent of the Year Award.

Susan Custer has been an active contributor to K–12 education for over thirty years. She has been recognized as a leader in supporting the implementation of professional learning communities for principals and is an exemplary principal coach.

Dr. Wendy Doty is superintendent of a large urban school district in Los Angeles County. She currently oversees over 22,000 students.

Dr. Wendy Dunlap was recently named Superintendent of the Year by Pepperdine University. She presently serves as superintendent of 16,300 students in grades 9–12.

Henry Escobar has been a superintendent for over fifteen years. He has received numerous awards and recognitions from private, civic, and educational organizations, including Local Educator of the Year and Superintendent of the Year for his region.

Dr. Dennis Fox has contributed to the field of education for over thirty-five years, serving as a teacher, principal, and consultant. He is best known for his extensive work with administrators and teachers in the practical use of data in decision making.

Robert Fraisse served as distinguished Educator in Residence at California Lutheran University between his positions as district superintendent. He currently serves as superintendent of a unified school district in Southern California.

Dr. Carmella Franco served in a midsize K–8 district for twelve years. She is currently serving as interim superintendent for a unified school district.

Dr. Jean Fuller served as a district superintendent prior to beginning her work in the California State Assembly. She is a strong proponent of public schools and frequently advocates for students in her work with the state assembly.

Roger Gallizzi serves as superintendent of a K–8 district of 28,000 students. He has been instrumental in building equity and understanding of the needs of language minority students throughout his district and region.

Tom Giampietro is the superintendent/principal of an elementary school district. His insights into the difficulty of performing a dual administrative role were most helpful.

Becci Gillespie has completed seven years as the superintendent of a K–8 district. Her honors include an award for Excellence in Special Education.

Dr. Gwen Gross served as superintendent for fifteen years in four different school districts. She has collaborated with seven other superintendents in co-authoring three books on the topic of leadership.

Dr. Jack Gyves spent over twenty-five years as a superintendent of schools, the largest of which served 32,000 students. He has been involved in recruiting, training, and mentoring superintendents in recent years.

Dr. Mimi Hennessey served as superintendent for nine years in the Arcadia Unified School District, a K–12 district of approximately 10,000 students.

Robert Hodges has served his current district for thirty-six years in a variety of capacities, including as superintendent since 1995. He currently counts among his many community activities a seat on the local hospital board.

Terri Lancaster is in her tenth year as a superintendent/principal. She previously taught for twelve years in the same district.

Dr. Ron Leon serves as mentor, coach, and trainer to other superintendents. He has been a district superintendent and a university instructor focused on teaching superintendents and other educational leaders.

Sandra Lyon has the unique experience of serving in a small, rural school district as both superintendent and principal. She was a consultant for an educational company that trained teachers and administrators before becoming a superintendent.

Dr. William Mathis has been a superintendent for over twenty-five years and was honored as the AASA Superintendent of the Year for Vermont in 2003. He was a finalist for AASA National Superintendent of the Year in 2003.

Dr. Sharon McGehee has served over 28,700 students in large districts for over eight years. She counts as one of her greatest achievements the creation of a strong staff development department to meet the needs of all employees, including the creation of Professional Learning Communities.

Ned McNabb was superintendent of a rural desert school district for over eight years. During that time he improved student safety, quality of instruction, and established an exemplary program for alternative education.

Dr. Gary Mekeel has served in two K–8 districts over the past seventeen years. His experience spans a very small district to a midsize one. He was honored by his colleagues as the Superintendent of the Year for his region.

Dr. Henry Mothner is the director of the Division for School Improvement at the Los Angeles County Office of Education. He created and oversees a division that specializes in addressing the needs of low-performing schools and districts.

Dr. Ken Noonan has extensive experience as a school district superintendent. He is a past president of the California State Board of Education.

Dr. Maria Ott has been superintendent of a district of 17,000 students for the past decade. She has received multiple awards and has worked as deputy superintendent of the Los Angeles Unified School District, the largest school district in California.

Sue Page was superintendent/principal of the smallest school district in Los Angeles County, California, at the time of the study. She has served in this role for four years. She recently had the unique task of overseeing a charter school with an enrollment that far exceeds the student count in her entire district.

Dr. Krista D. Parent has been a superintendent for over eight years. She was the AASA 2007 National Superintendent of the Year, the first superintendent from the state of Oregon to be so honored. Dr. Parent is the chair of Oregon's Assessing Leadership Performance Workgroup.

Dr. James Phares was the 2007 AASA West Virginia Superintendent of the Year and a national finalist for the Superintendent of the Year honors. He has been a superintendent for ten years in a district serving over 8,100 students.

Dr. Juli Quinn has served for thirty-six years in public education, the last three as director, Regional System of District and School Support Region 11. She and her staff strive to provide quality service and solutions to help school districts close the achievement gap.

Dr. Sharon Robison was a superintendent for seven years in a K–12 district of 19,000 students. Upon her retirement, the board of education rededicated the school district's administrative complex, naming it the Sharon S. Robison Administrative Center.

Dr. Darline Robles is the county superintendent in Los Angeles County. She is responsible for providing oversight to districts and programs spanning a large geographic area of Southern California. Prior to that she served as a district superintendent in a large school district.

Dr. Beverly Rohrer began her work as a school superintendent in 1990. She has been the superintendent of several large urban school districts and is well known for her volunteer service to community, youth, and other nonprofit organizations.

Regina Rossall has over thirty years of experience in the field of education. She currently serves as district superintendent in a K–8 district and works as a part-time university professor providing instruction to educators entering the field.

Sherry Smith has fourteen years of experience as superintendent in two districts. She currently serves a high school district. She was honored by her colleagues in 2007 as Superintendent of the Year for her region.

Dr. Howard Sundberg is relatively new to the superintendency but has been an educator for thirty-five years. He currently serves in a midsize urban school district. He is involved in his local community and in professional organizations in his area.

Dr. Louise Taylor served as a superintendent for over seventeen years in a midsize district. Most of her schools were honored as California Distinguished Schools during her superintendency.

Sandra Thorstenson has been superintendent of a 9–12 district of over 13,500 students for seven years. She was named Superintendent of the Year for her region in 2008.

Dr. Rene Townsend spent ten years as superintendent in two districts that spanned Pre-K to Grade 12. One of her districts served 3,000 students, the other 25,000. She is the co-author of four leadership books.

Dr. David J. Verdugo has over three years of experience serving students in grades K–12. He was chosen as Superintendent of the Year for his region in 2008.

Dr. Jim Vidak has over the past seventeen years been elected as the Tulare County superintendent of schools. He is currently serving his fifth term in office.

Dr. David Vierra is in his eighth year as the superintendent of a large 9–12 district. He was the recipient of the Claremont Graduate University Urban Leadership Award in 2003.

Renee Whitson has served her school district for over thirteen years. She was named the Association of California School Administrators Region XI Superintendent of the Year. She has also been honored as Exeter's Woman of the Year.

Dr. Marc Winger has been a K–6 superintendent for over seven years. He is known as an advocate for public education and a proponent for positive change on behalf of students. He was recognized by his peers as Superintendent of the Year for his region in 2005.

Dr. Roberta Zapf has extensive experience as an educator. She worked as a curriculum director and served as a superintendent of schools in Southern California. Dr. Zapf has extensive experience in the public arena and has been a vital force for change in California.

Breinigsville, PA USA
22 September 2010
245803BV00003B/6/P

9 781607 097211